THE LAST ONE'S GONE

LOST RAILWAY LOCATIONS OF THE 1960s

Keith Widdowson

AMBERLEY

First published 2020

Amberley Publishing
The Hill, Stroud
Gloucestershire, GL5 4EP

www.amberley-books.com

British Library Cataloguing in Publication Data.
A catalogue record for this book is available from the British Library.

ISBN 978 1 4456 9597 6 (print)
ISBN 978 1 4456 9598 3 (ebook)

Typeset in 10.5pt on 13pt Sabon.
Typesetting by Aura Technology and Software Services, India.
Printed in the UK.

CONTENTS

Introduction

I believe the major catalyst for the decline in railway travel throughout the '50s was the combination of both increasing affluence (Harold Macmillan's 1957 statement 'You've never had it so good'), thus allowing families to spend their rising income on car ownership, and the two-week 1955 ASLEF strike, compelling intending travellers to make alternative arrangements, many never returning to rail. With BR falling into serious deficit, the Conservative government appointed, from ICI, Dr Richard Beeching to resolve the matter. His 1963 *Reshaping of British Railways* proposed the closure of nearly 5,000 miles of track together with in excess of 2,300 stations. In February '64 the then Transport Minister, Ernest Marples, made one concession – promising to close no seaside branch lines before October that year, so people could plan their summer holidays for that summer. The election in October 1964 bought in a Labour government whose manifesto 'promised' to stop the railway closures. This was reneged upon and Barbara Castle indeed saw to it that the largest closures of them all – the S&D and the GC – were authorised by her.

The comedy song-writing duo Michael Flanders and Donald Swan caught the mood of the nation with their 'Slow Train', mourning the closure of all those wonderfully named local stations that were to lose their train services, some of which I was lucky enough to visit during my five years of dashing around the country. Even the Poet Laureate of the time, Sir John Betjeman, made a number of short documentary journeys on Britain's fast disappearing branch lines, eulogising their uniqueness and the fast disappearing slow pace of life.

Here, therefore, dear reader, I offer up a personal travelogue of such locations I encountered on my voyages – before motorways scarred the landscape and passengers looked out of their train windows (rather than at their iPhones) at the wonderful vista Britain has to offer. I will never claim it as being a comprehensive collection; my priorities morphing, in 1965, to hunting down the fast dwindling steam-powered passenger trains, often to the detriment of DMU/DL-operated lines under the axe.

Route Miles Closed

1963	324	1964	1058	1965	600
1966	750	1967	300	1968	400
1969	250	1970	275	1971	23
1972	50	1973	35	1974	0

Note – dates are when railway lines closed to passenger trains, many often lingering on with freight.

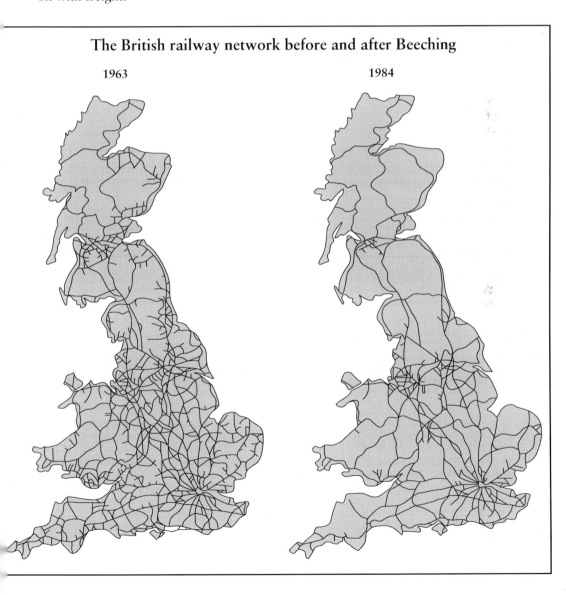

The British railway network before and after Beeching

1963   1984

The Brownie Phase

Upon joining British Railways as a telephone enquiry clerk at Waterloo in 1962, I soon found myself often in the presence of colleagues who had deliberately gained employment within BR for the sole purpose of utilising the associated travel perks in order to pursue their hobby: railway enthusiasm. Initially unaware of the widespread line closures proposed within the 1963 Beeching Axe but encouraged by others to get out there before it was too late, I began tentatively exploring my home region – the Southern. It sure was a different world away from my Kent-orientated daily commuter journey. Equipped with a Brownie 127 and a map extracted from the rear of the cumbersomely green-covered SR timetable (on which I coloured in the lines travelled over), this then sixteen-year-old teenager began what was to morph into a five-year adventure of travelling and living even on trains throughout Britain, homing in on line closures, as often detailed in the office copy of *The Railway World* magazine. As the office 'gopher', one of my duties was to visit the publicity cavern deep beneath Waterloo concourse. Here all the regional posters and handbills were stored and, with my interest in closing lines burgeoning, a copy of each closure notice fell into my hands. For many years these were stored away in my loft but, in the mid-'90s, with a financial crisis looming, I sold a lot of my railway mementos to make ends meet – the closure notices being very much in demand!

During that first year of my travels I foolishly failed to document either the trains travelled on or what was up front. It does appear that through throwing together several photographs I must, in the July of '63, having taken a half day's annual leave, travelled from my workplace at Waterloo to Reading. Probably having taken information from more experienced steam devotees, I then journeyed via Guildford and Horsham to Brighton. After walking up the steep Terminus Road, in order to take a panoramic view of Brighton shed, I headed home on the once daily DL-hauled 18.53 departure for Victoria, a service routed via Lewes, Eridge and Oxted – the section south of Uckfield being closed in 1969.

Holidaying in the West Country each year with my parents and brother usually meant getting up at the crack of dawn and suffering the lengthy delays along the A303 and A30, including the notorious bottleneck of the Exeter bypass. In the August of '63, perhaps flaunting my increasing independence (not to mention my free pass employment perk), I chose to travel to North Devon by train.

July 1963

Initially just Reading when opened by the SE&CR, this station was renamed Reading (South) in 1949 to differentiate it from the adjacent former GWR station. A further change to Reading (Southern) was made twelve years later, in 1965, before dieselisation of the Redhill line trains and electrification of a bay platform at the former GWR station, thus permitting the SR services to be diverted there. The site is now occupied by roads, roundabouts and offices. Did this BR Standard 4MT take me to Guildford that day? With no notes having been taken, who can say?

11 February 1964

Deputising for a shortage of fit DLs, No. 6856 *Stowe Grange* departs Reading (General) with the 12.05 Hereford to Paddington. The Southern station can be seen in the background.

7 August 1964
Reading train crews had one return working per day to/from Redhill. Having departed out of Reading at 06.50 that morning, No. 7829 *Ramsbury Manor* is caught reversing out of Reading (Southern), en route to the depot, having returned in with the 11.35 from Redhill. The equivalent Saturday working was a Hymeck DL (Class 35).

July 1963
Making my way from Guildford to Horsham we cross Ivatt 2-6-4T No. 41327, working a Guildford-bound train at Cranleigh.

July 1963
A poor Brownie shot of Brighton shed taken from Howard Place – a once well-trodden route
to the BRSA Club, where I had many meetings with Brighton drivers' union representatives.
Although only tank locomotives of the Ivatt and Standard types can be seen, a handful of
Bulleid West Countries, Maunsell Ns and Terriers were still allocated there at the time. Well
worth a visit is www.thebrightonmotivepowerdepots.yolasite.com for stories of/from the
men who worked there.

I well remember queuing under the triangular sign hanging above the concourse
at Waterloo, waiting in a lengthy line for the designated train to be platformed.
Once again failing to record the locomotives involved, upon eventually arriving
at Mortehoe, my father, having already arrived at the Woolacombe holiday camp,
popped back the short distance to pick me up. Returning via the same method, at
least I took a couple of photographs at Mortehoe station whilst waiting for my
London-bound train.

That September, aware of the imminent closure of the electrified Haywards
Heath to Horsted Keynes via Ardingly line, I travelled over it to visit the
embryonic Bluebell Railway. The only other outing that year was in October to
the Hayling Island branch – a line that was to close a week later. Initially oblivious
to its uniqueness, as regards the use of the diminutive A1X Terriers employed
on the trains, it was not only to prove a catalyst for my penchant to travel over
railway routes that were doomed under the Beeching Axe, but would morph into
a nationwide hunt to travel with as many steam locomotives as possible, prior
to their unnecessary early annihilation. Following that visit, more by luck than
judgement, I went on to cover every SR closure, excepting the DEMU-operated
Sprat & Winkle line between Andover Junction and Romsey, after that date.

August 1963
Whilst waiting for my home-going Waterloo-bound Mortehoe and Woolacombe service, the 06.20 Taunton to Ilfracombe arrived with GWR Mogul No. 7337 at its head.

No. 7337 was assisted up the 1 in 40 Mortehoe bank by No. 31842 at the rear. From 1990 to 2004 the station was used as a basis for a children's theme park. Subsequently developed as a housing estate, the main station buildings and platform, next to which the Tarka Trail footpath passes, remain intact.

26 October 1963
The substantial costs associated with remedying the deteriorating condition of the 1,100-ft-long, weight-restricted timber swing-bridge that crossed Langstone Harbour led to the 4½-mile-line being closed. Just a week prior to its cessation and the subsequently preserved Terrier A1X 0-6-0T No. 32650 is seen in the bay platform at Havant. Today, the area where the tracks once stood on the Havant side of the line is a nature reserve and footpath, enabling users to walk from Havant station all the way to where the bridge and the level crossing were located, at Langstone. On the island itself, the majority of the track bed has been used as part of the Hayling Billy cycling/footpath trail.

November 1963
The one-time terminus of a 4¾-mile branch line at Westerham, from the main line station of Dunton Green, was photographed on a Sunday morning cycle ride. Strong objections to the original closure date of 1960 merely gave the line a further twelve months – the last trains running in October 1961. Most of the route has been buried under the M25. As a nod to the line's Westerham Flyer sobriquet, an industrial site named Flyers Way now occupies the former station site.

1964

One wet Saturday in the March of '64 saw me make my first recorded journey behind steam – the honour falling to BR Standard 4MT No. 80140 working the 13.56 Tonbridge to Eastbourne. I was en route to a Sussex YHA and, with the DEMU fleet underutilised on a Sunday, the return trip was in one of them too.

Later that month I embarked on my very first overnight train journey en route to Wales. Little did I realise, at that time, the advantages of overnight travel – enabling one to arrive into an area earlier, rather than late in the morning, thus allowing a whole day's travels there. Indeed, over the following four years over 300 nights were spent on trains or platforms throughout Britain. My minder, Bill, had suggested a visit to Wales in order to travel over the doomed Neath to Pontypool Road line. It was, retrospectively, his enthusiasm that perhaps provided the catalyst for my life-long interest in railways, or more pertinently, steam. Bill had planned it all – I just tagged along. Suitably equipped with extra paraphernalia, not previously taken with me on daytime trips, namely, a toothbrush, flannel, and large(r) supplies of food, I met Bill on Paddington's Lawn just gone midnight on Saturday morning, the 20th. We were to catch the unusually routed (via Gloucester) 01.00 departure for Swansea. Noise associated with long station stops, while BR and GPO staff off-loaded papers and mail traffic, meant only intermittent sleep was obtained during the six and a half hour, 126-mile journey, Hymeck diesel-hydraulic D7026 depositing us at Swansea just gone 07.30.

The western end of the line we were to travel over that day was constructed by the Vale of Neath Railway and opened in 1851 and, although the Taff Vale Extension of the Newport, Abergavenny & Hereford Railway from Pontypool Road to Quakers Yard was opened in 1858, it was a further six years before the connecting link between the two railways, at Middle Duffren Junction, was accomplished. Constructed along the head of most valleys, during the line's heyday it was exceptionally busy – the connections with numerous other valley lines heavily contributing to its usefulness. As the coal mining industry declined during the '50s and '60s, so did the line's usage, and in June '64 the line closed to passengers, various small sections lingering on for freight traffic a few more years.

Two and a quarter hours later, at 13.20, we finally arrived at Pontypool Road and headed the short distance to Newport, before retracing our outward route all the way back, via Gloucester, to the Golden Valley junction station of Kemble. We were

21 March 1964
Enough station time here allowed me to alight at Hirwaun and take a hurried shot of Collett 0-6-2T No. 5659 at the head of our 11.05 Neath to Pontypool Road train. Until recent times, freight continued to use the line. A proposal for the reinstatement of rail services from Aberdare, 3½ miles distant, is under discussion.

The highlight, of course, was crossing Britain's highest railway viaduct – the 200-ft-high, 284-yard-long, Crumlin viaduct – at a speed restricted 20 mph. Although of historic value, due to its perilous condition the decision was made to dismantle it. The process took nine months and was completed in February 1967.

there that evening because the two branch lines, to Tetbury and Cirencester, were to close the following month.

The 1843-built Swindon to Cheltenham line opened with a provision of a station at Tetbury Road. As this was 7 miles from Tetbury itself, the town's residents felt they were losing out on the benefits rail connection would bring and, in 1863, proposed a connecting railway be built. It was an astonishing twenty-six years, following contractors going broke and financial difficulties, before the line was opened. In contrast, the Cirencester branch was a far easier build. Proposed in 1836, and opened five years later, the station was renamed Cirencester Town in 1924 to differentiate it from the M&SWJR station at Cirencester Watersmeet.

Dusk was now falling as we boarded the 17.00 Tetbury branch departure. This was my first occasion of travelling in one of the German-built railbuses. The bouncing, wheel-screeching and shuddering vibrations whilst rounding corners had to be experienced to be believed. After a lengthy thirty-four-minute turnaround, we returned to Kemble, crossing the footbridge to join the Cirencester train, which was to depart from its dedicated bay. In contrast to our Tetbury stop, the turnaround

21 March 1964
In fading light, 1959-built A. C. four-wheel railbus No. W79977 stands at Tetbury having arrived with the 17.00 from Kemble, two weeks prior to the line's closure. Three of these forty-six seat A. C. built railbuses replaced steam on both this and the Cirencester branch during 1959. Dieselisation, however, failed to stem the mounting losses. On the last day of April, a coffin was loaded onto the final train at Trouble House Halt, having been delayed by burning hay bales placed on the track by protesters. It was addressed to Dr Beeching and was to be forwarded from Kemble to Paddington. The only remaining building is the Staffordshire blue brick-built goods shed, which has been converted into an arts centre.

at Cirencester was a mere six minutes, and we were soon heading back to London behind our third Hymeck of the day, D7040. Our mission completed, we arrived into Paddington at the not unreasonable time of 21.00. Having experienced the advantage of overnight travel, I decided that it was the way forward with my newly realized hobby – to visit parts of Britain hitherto unexplored by me.

I was now avidly scouring the office copy of *The Railway World* magazine in order to travel over lines due for imminent closure and, to this end, the week later saw me head off to another part of Great Britain never before visited – East Anglia – in order to travel over the doomed former M&GNR stub west of Sheringham.

Into April and, now equipped with a modern Kodak Colorsnap 135, a convoluted figure eight itinerary was undertaken to travel over a series of lines closing the following week. Catching the West of England 01.15 departure out of Waterloo, I alighted at Salisbury, connecting onto a 03.17 Salisbury to Weymouth train. A wonderful moonlit 58-mile journey via Verwood, Wimborne, Broadstone and Wareham taking all of two and a half hours, newspapers and mails being offloaded en route, was enjoyed. After a breakfast in a local café I caught the 06.35 out of Weymouth which, having back-tracked over the same route to West Moors, then headed through the New Forest to Brockenhurst over the original Castleman's Corkscrew (so called after the promoter, Wimborne Solicitor Charles Castleman,

28 March 1964
Once the engineering hub HQ of the 150-mile M&GNR system, but now its last remaining truncated stub. In its penultimate week of existence, the 14.12 from Norwich stands at the deserted platforms of Melton Constable. The station was demolished in 1971, to be replaced by a telephone exchange. Two of the ornamental spandrels that held up the station roof are incorporated into the bus shelter on the B1354 Fakenham Road. The land of the old railway works and sidings is now an industrial estate, but a number of the old buildings have been retained. As an aside, on the journey there, I espied, at North Walsham, a closure notice for the 5-mile Mundesley-on-Sea branch (1898 to October 1964) and, en route back to London, alighted there, to travel over it.

My faithful Kodak Colorsnap 135 – a seventeenth birthday present from my parents.

25 April 1964
A double whammy was to affect train services here at Wimborne. Until 1885 it was a reversal station for trains off the S&D and then, three years later, the New Forest cut off opened, allowing Bournemouth trains from London to run on a more direct route via Christchurch, thus relegating this line to a secondary status. The 06.35 Weymouth to Brockenhurst calls there a week before closure with one of Bournemouth's competent Standard 2-6-0s, No. 76026, in charge. The site is nowadays partially occupied by the weekly market – commercial units covering the remainder.

25 April 1964

Although Bournemouth shed was bunked twice whilst waiting for trains at the nearby Central station, the best photographic opportunities were always available from the lengthy Down platform. Seen here resting between duties is Merchant Navy Pacific No. 35023 *Holland-Afrika Line* – one of the locomotives behind which 100+ mph speeds were achieved during the gung-ho spring of '67.

11 March 1967

Now bereft of her nameplates, rebuilt BoB No. 34087 *145 Squadron*, whose claim to fame was working the last steam-hauled Up TPO (22.13 Weymouth to Waterloo) that July, just fits on the 65 ft turntable.

3 June 1967
Preserved A4 No. 4498 *Sir Nigel Gresley* is being serviced whilst working a railtour. The entire site is now a car park, over which the dual carriage A338 Wessex Way noisily sours the area.

25 April 1964
My first of an eventual four visits to the S&D was in April '64 on the 11.40 Bournemouth West to Bristol Temple Meads. On that occasion, the subsequently preserved LMS 4F 0-6-0 No. 44422 was in charge, seen here departing Evercreech Junction.

together with the meandering nature of the line) main line. After then making my way to Bournemouth, I headed north over the S&D, changing at Evercreech Junction onto its former main line to Highbridge. The Poet Laureate John Betjeman once eulogised about his journey along this route as idyllic and nostalgic, words which don't sit well with the accountants, and it was plain to see the WR had abandoned any hope of longevity for the system. The Collett-designed 0-6-0 No. 2218, minus her brass cab side number plates, as well as her smoke box equivalent, dawdled along, taking just under an hour for the 22½-mile journey, with her one-coach, one-van train calling at all stations for the non-existent passengers. If ever, years later, there was a perfect scenario to remember, this, with its country stations and remote junctions, was it. It's as if it was a throwback to a stress-free life, long since disappeared. If only I'd appreciated it back then. I wasn't to know that ahead of me lay over forty years of London commuting with all its attendant trials and tribulations! Perhaps bucking against the trend, recalling my travels throughout the mid-sixties, my teenage years, rather than my schooldays, were the best years of my life.

The next condemned line I was now heading for was the 26-mile-long Somerset Levels line between Taunton and Yeovil. Sleep deprivation now caught up with me and, having overslept my original alighting point of Yeovil Town, a fortunate eight-minute connection at Pen Mill returned me there in time to get the auto train to the Junction and homeward bound to London.

25 April 1964
We now move on to Taunton, where we see 2-6-0 U No. 31792 preparing to work that day's 16.25 departure, via Langport and Martock, to her home depot of Yeovil. This 20-mile line, opened by the Bristol & Exeter Railway in 1853, was Yeovil's first railway and was constructed across a flood plain, the rivers Parrett and Yeo never being far away. With its stations some distance from the villages they purported to serve, it was inevitable that any prospective passengers found the frequent local bus services more convenient, closure being just weeks away. Part of the track bed has subsequently been used for the A3088 – a connecting road from Yeovil to the A303, the popular partially dual carriageway route to the West of England.

Aware that the trains operating services over the Adur Valley line (Sussex) were being dieselised that May, an eventually abandoned attempt (heavy rain) thwarted a trip over it – a couple of shots of the Ivatt tank-hauled trains taken from the station shelters at Hove and Shoreham-by-Sea.

Next up and my line manager at Waterloo, having informed me that the elderly M7s were being withdrawn in the near future, released me from my duties half an hour early one Saturday that May, sending me to catch runs with them on the push-pull-operated Lymington and Swanage branches, calling in at Bournemouth West en route. I was now becoming more mindful of various line closures and, to this effect, on the last Tuesday that same month, both the Staines West branch and the Sturt Lane Chord (Brookwood to Frimley) were part of a nine-hour marathon of lines covered. The following day, Sussex was my destination and, after first catching one of Redhill's Standard 4MTs on the Tunbridge Wells West to East Grinstead High Level line, I accessed the Cuckoo line, via Hurst Green, following a series of either DEMU or Type 3 (Class 33) services, finally catching a steam train into Eastbourne. Taking a Southdown bus over the scenic Downs themselves to Seaford, I headed for Bexhill – the final doomed line of the day being the 4½-mile Bexhill West branch from Crowhurst.

Into July and I turned my attention to the former L&SWR's Withered Arm network of lines west of Exeter. The double whammy of the Beeching Axe and the Western Region's inheritance of these lines, under the 1963 boundary changes,

28 April 1964
Although Hove station is still extant, everything else shown here isn't. The semaphores, the locomotive and the coaching stock, together with the Adur Valley line the train was to travel over have all gone. Ivatt 2-6-2T No. 41299 approaches with the 11.37 Brighton to Horsham – the Adur line services being turned over to DEMUs with the summer timetable changes just weeks later. Previously called Cliftonville, the station acquired its final name of Hove in 1895.

9 May 1964

The syncopated panting associated with the fifty-nine-year-old's Westinghouse brake fills the air at Lymington Pier, having stalled on a minor climb on the outward journey, as she waits departure time with the 14.20 for Brockenhurst. This elderly tank (*c.* 1905), M7 No. 30052, was to be, along with the half a dozen other remaining members, withdrawn by the month's end. The station canopy has long gone, prospective passengers off the Yarmouth ferry having to take refuge from the Solent winds within one of the bus shelters situated along the open concrete platform.

9 May 1964

The last days of the veteran SR 0-4-4T M7 tanks and, by default, push-pull operation on the SR, sees Bournemouth's No. 30107 about to work the 17.38 departure from Swanage for Wareham. With DEMUs having taken over from the September of '66, BR, in 1968, citing a shortage of stock, proposed the closure of the line – a vociferous campaign by locals merely obtained a four-year extension of life for the branch. Reopened by the Swanage Railway preservation group in 1982, the line is now an intrinsic part of the Isle of Purbeck tourist industry.

9 May 1964
Bournemouth West was the resort's first station – London-bound trains initially having to run west via Poole and Ringwood. A lifelong Bath Green Park resident, Standard 5MT No. 73051 readies for departure with the 15.40 for Bristol Temple Meads. The WR's penchant for applying a green livery to their Standard 5MTs when visiting Swindon for overhaul gave them, in my opinion, an aesthetically improved appearance.

3 July 1965
Fast-forward to the July of '65 and Standard Mogul No. 76057 makes a thunderous departure with the 18.48 for Templecombe. After Bournemouth West's closure, most S&D services were truncated at Branksome, until the line's demise in March 1966. Initially closed due to engineering work in connection with the Bournemouth line electrification in September 1965, with a replacement bus service to boot, BR realised that, although more convenient for the town centre and beaches, they needn't reopen it – permanent closure being enacted the following month. The station was demolished shortly after closure with the area now hidden under a car park and the A338 Wessex Way dual carriageway. Bournemouth Traincare Depot occupies the former approaches to the station.

26 May 1964

As part of a convoluted plan compiled to encompass travelling over both Windsor branches and several Surrey and Middlesex suburban routes, I found myself at Staines West ready to travel over the 6¼-mile branch to the WR main line station, at West Drayton. AEC-powered Pressed Steel single railcar No. W55024 formed the 15.28 departure that day. Due to the area it served being sparsely populated, passenger expectations never fully materialised. Built on the River Colne flood plain and surrounded by both the Staines and Wraysbury reservoirs, it was proposed for closure under the 1963 Beeching Axe, subsequently closing in March '65. The station building survives and has been converted into commercial offices. The platform and adjacent tracks have been replaced with a car park.

27 May 1964

Unsure of which services along the Cuckoo line were steam-operated, my first trip over it was on a DEMU. I passed Brighton-allocated N No. 31866 at Heathfield with the 11.45 Eastbourne to Tonbridge. The line north of Hailsham closed in 1965, the truncated stub from Polegate surviving until 1968. The tunnel north of the station is now a lit cycle track, whilst the only remaining station building is the street level former booking office, which nowadays a shop/café.

27 May 1964
Bexhill West was opened by the SE&CR in a bid to cream off the lucrative day-tripper market from the rival LB&SCR, but being far less conveniently sited the station never achieved its expectations. The grandiose station, once boasting four platforms, stands deserted three weeks before closure, the 18.45 for Crowhurst awaiting non-existent patronage. Awarded a Grade II listed status, the station buildings are now an antique shop, whilst the former refreshment room is now a public house/restaurant.

boded ill for them – only the three-month seasonal summer peaks witnessed high passenger usage. An additional nail in the coffin was the fact that the aforementioned peaks required a considerable quantity of coaching stock, which not only remained dormant between weekends but also for the majority of the other nine months of the year. Within the Beeching Report was the fact that the all-year maintenance of those vehicles outweighed the income generated and, to save costs, they should therefore be withdrawn. Taking all this into consideration, for two consecutive Saturday mornings that July I departed Waterloo on the 00.45 wavy-lined service to the West of England. A timetable entry with a wavy line running through it indicated that it didn't run for all of the period of the timetable's validity and reference had to be made, aided by a notation at the column head, as to the precise dates of operation. On the first occasion I travelled to the extremity of the former L&SWR system, Padstow, returning east via Bodmin Road and the GWML to Exeter. After then encompassing the Exmouth, Seaton and Lyme Regis branches, I completed this 600-mile trip sleeping soundly en route home to the 'smoke'.

On the second occasion I headed to the Atlantic coast resorts of Bude and Ilfracombe, travelling between them over the 1925-opened North Devon & Cornwall Light Railway line between Halwill and Torrington. That entire day's travel was centred around this line – the sparse service of two trains a day being somewhat problematic to encompass. Having said that, it really was the highlight of my West Country travels. The one-coach train wound its way through the picturesque North

11 July 1964

Withdrawn from her home shed of Exmouth Junction two months later, forty-year-old N No. 31840 waits (in typical West Country weather) in the bay platform at Okehampton to work the 06.25 (a portion off the 01.10 Waterloo to Plymouth) for Padstow. Initially, Okehampton residents were overjoyed at having escaped the '60s slaughter of railways in Devon. However, the end came as late as 1972. It was reopened in 1997 for a limited Sundays only service from Exeter to Okehampton station. The axis of the Dartmoor Railway preservation group also run services to Meldon.

11 July 1964

It's 07.30 in the morning and, after a memorable seven-hour 260-mile journey from London, BoB No. 34054 *Lord Beaverbrook* (which had worked the train from Exeter) is seen at Padstow resting from her exertions, surrounded by sea mist, at this almost beachside station. Through services from London, including the Atlantic Coast Express, were to cease that September – the North Cornwall route, via Halwill, closing in October '66 and the residual Bodmin branch services being withdrawn in January '67. The station building is extant and in use by Padstow Town Council as offices, whilst the trackbed into the town is now part of the Camel Trail.

11 July 1964

I then took the 08.12 Bodmin Road train espying, at Wadebridge, a diminutive pannier tank simmering in the sidings. It was one of the six examples of Collett's 1F 0-6-0PTs, thirty-year-old No. 1369. It had arrived there in 1962 from duties on the Weymouth Quay branch, itself displacing the Beattie tanks on the weight-restricted Wenford Bridge china clay branch. Although withdrawn that autumn, she survives today on the South Devon Railway. The main station building still stands and is in use as the John Betjeman Centre. A road, compassionately called Southern Way, runs along the old track bed where the main platform was. The engine shed area is now a housing estate, and the sand dock is now a Co-op store.

11 July 1964

Until 1933, Exeter Central was called Queen Street, and is included in this book because of its once pivotal status for West of England-bound trains from Waterloo. The lengthy London trains were reduced to portions for their onward journeys to the Devon and Cornwall seaside resorts. Due to their weight, the Merchant Navys were banned west of here. This scene shows No. 35009 *Shaw Savill Line* preparing to depart for Waterloo in the final summer of such services. Whilst the station is extant, both through roads have given way to an excess of foliage.

11 July 1964

That summer the sole remaining loco-hauled departure, seen here with BR 3MT No. 82042 waiting time, out of the then four-platformed Exmouth was the 13.34 (via Budleigh Salterton) portion for Sidmouth Junction, where it was combined with the 14.02 portion from Sidmouth en route to Waterloo. At Exmouth, following the closure of the Budleigh Salterton line, the remaining trains (from Exeter) then terminated in the truncated former platform 2. The eastern side of the station is now a road, a bus station and leisure centre having been built on the former main station site.

11 July 1964

The 11.48 Plymouth to Waterloo is seen arriving into Sidmouth Junction having been taken over at Exeter Central by Merchant Navy No. 35019 *French Line CGT*. Closed along with the Sidmouth branch, in March of '67 it was reopened as Feniton (the original name until it became a junction station in 1874) in 1971 to serve the large newly constructed nearby housing estate. The platform I was standing on in 1964 remains disused, the single line through the station using the original Down platform.

11 July 1964

Originally named Colyton-for-Seaton, Seaton Junction opened on 19 July 1860 on completion of the Exeter Extension of the L&SWR west of Yeovil. With the opening of the Seaton & Beer Railway in 1868, the name was changed to Colyton Junction, before finally becoming Seaton Junction the following year. Originally, trains arriving from the Seaton branch had to reverse into the Down (westbound) platform. However, the station was reconstructed in 1927/8 with two through tracks on the main line and loops to the newly extended platforms. At the same time a new branch line platform was added, set at an angle of 45° to the main line. One of the three Exmouth Junction BR 4MTs, No. 75022, awaits in the Up platform for a path back to her depot.

11 July 1964

BoB No. 34070 *Manston* arrives into Seaton Junction with the 15.35 stopping service from Exeter Central to Salisbury. These stopping services were anathema to Beeching and, sure enough, with many of the less well-patronised stations over this route being closed within months, trains such as this ceased to run. The station buildings are nowadays a private residence; however, the concrete footbridge, over which I crossed to connect into the branch line train, still straddles the line.

11 July 1964

At Seaton the 16.00 departure for Seaton Junction waits for custom on a very warm July '64 day. Closed in 1966, the majority of the 4¼-mile track bed is now used by the Seaton Tramway, most of the former station site nowadays being occupied by the tramway's maintenance depot.

11 July 1964

A wonderfully engineered 6¾-mile line, the majority of which ran through Devon, actually terminated here at the Dorset seaside town of Lyme Regis and was for many years the preserve of the unique Adams Radial tanks. Here, the train I was on that day, the 17.15 for Axminster, was to suffer a ninenteen-minute delay whilst the driver rectified a fault. The station building survives, albeit having been removed to Alresford on the Mid Hants Preserved line, whilst industrial units now occupy the site.

14 August 1966

The subsequently preserved Peppercorn Pacific No. 60532 *Blue Peter* calls at Axminster whilst working the A2 Commemorative Railtour – she wasn't a very well bunny, temporarily failing whilst climbing Honiton bank. This shot is included because one can see, in front of the locomotive, the incline of the now closed Lyme Regis branch, necessary to cross the main line.

18 July 1964

After arriving into Bude just minutes earlier and having espied a photographic opportunity on an embankment opposite the signal box, I yomped, case and camera in hand, hell for leather to obtain a photograph of it. BR Standard 4MT No. 80042 departs with the 07.58 for Okehampton. Nothing remains of the station today, although a nearby street of sheltered housing has been sympathetically named Bulleid Way.

18 July 1964

Maunsell-designed N No. 31849 arrives into Halwill with the 08.10 Wadebridge to Waterloo – the Bude portion is in the distance, ready to be attached at the rear. The small platform to the right was for the twice-daily ND&CJR Torrington bound trains. To commemorate the station's former (1887–1923) name, that of junction, the surrounding area is now so called; a nearby public house is named the Junction Inn. Although little remains of the station, the track bed is now a cycle way. Several nearby roads are called Station Field, Station High Road and, unbelievably, Beeching Close.

18 July 1964

Having taken just under 1½ hours to travel the 20½ miles over the former ND&CJR with the one-coach 10.52 from Halwill, Ivatt No. 41249 is seen recuperating from her exertions after arrival at Torrington. The station buildings are now the Puffing Billy licensed restaurant, whilst the Tarka Valley Railway has an assortment of stock berthed in the adjacent platform.

Devon countryside, stopping at all the stations (in reality either several concrete slabs or planks of wood) and level crossings – the latter because all were ungated, the guard having to alight, walk forward, see the train across and rejoin. Built as late as 1925 to optimistically open up the area to tourism and help both farmers and the china clay industry, the line, not aided by the meagre passenger train service, failed to achieve any viability. The train schedules, restricted to 20 mph as the line was classified as a light railway, allowed for time at a number of stations to attach/detach goods wagons as required – when none were forthcoming, the train crew occupied the time with a game of cards! At Torrington, the SR dual-classed carriage, provided perhaps in the unlikely event of First Class clientele, was exchanged for a WR two-coach set for the remaining 14 miles to North Devon's most populous town of Barnstaple. After then, taking a return trip to Ilfracombe, a wonderfully scenic crossing of Exmoor was enjoyed prior to, from Taunton, a journey home over the then novelty of CWR (continuous welded rail) to Paddington.

Closer to home (Kent being my residence), I subjected myself to an uncomfortably hot 77-mile, three-hour ride in a DMU over the Cambridge to Oxford Varsity line. Although not included within Beeching's plan, notices for closure had been published. Perhaps being a glutton for punishment, further DMU travels were undertaken later that month on the Eastern Region. Although the priority was the doomed Buntingford branch, Enfield Town, Hertford East and North Woolwich locations were also in the mix.

18 July 1964
The opportunity to take this shot at Dulverton arose from the train I was on having to wait on the single line for the westbound train, the 16.03 Taunton to Barnstaple Junction with Mogul No. 6326 in charge, to cross. Note the former Exe Valley bay platform on the right, services over which had ceased the previous year. The former station buildings are now a private residence.

25 July 1964
A five-hour-long bash of the ER branch lines, predominantly in order to travel over the Buntingford branch, was undertaken one hot and sunny Saturday in July '64. At Buntingford the 12.25 St Margaret's departure, with just myself and the lone passenger seen boarding, waits time. The station building survives as a private residence.

That year's annual family holiday was at Totland on the Isle of Wight and, after waving goodbye to my family at Yarmouth, who were returning home by car via Lymington, I caught a Southern Vectis bus to Newport. After a four-hour step into the Edwardian time warp the island's railways appeared to exist in and following a bouncy 4-COR ride up the Portsmouth Direct, I reunited with them later that day.

Onto August, and a week-long stay with my father's Leicester relations facilitated me to home in on a number of lines which weren't to see the year out. Staying in a B&B at Preston en route allowed me travel over all the Fylde lines including Blackpool Central, the Fleetwood branch and the Marton Direct. Initially taking the opportunity to call in the local establishments of Leicester Midland shed and the closed station of West Bridge, on the Tuesday I ventured out to the doomed Derby Friargate branch from Nottingham Victoria, returning back to my base via the steam-operated Stamford/Seaton push/pull-operated line – the latter being dieselised in 1965 and closed in 1966.

The following day I made my first visit to Birmingham. Travelling via Nuneaton into Birmingham New Street and aided by the street directions contained within Lt Aiden Fuller's well-thumbed *Locoshed Book*, I walked the short distance to Snow Hill. Although the GWML from Paddington to Chester had, in the 1963 boundary changes, been awarded to the LMR north of Aynho Junction, Snow Hill was still very much steeped in its former owner's paraphernalia and atmosphere. Opened in 1852 by the GWR, it was initially just named Birmingham, then Great Charles Street,

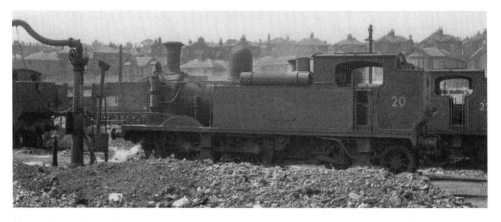

15 August 1964

The one-time northern terminus of the Isle of Wight railways (north thereof being a tramway). Ryde St Johns Road motive power depot was situated on the west side of the line, easily accessible off the northbound platform. With the summer service in full swing, I was surprised to see any of the sixteen remaining aged O2s there – the detritus of a working steam shed being seen here to good advantage.

15 August 1964

This photograph is included as a perfect example of the wonder of the bubble that the Edwardian Isle of Wight trains lived in. The 15.10 Ryde Pier Head to Shanklin, a summer Saturday extra to cope with demand, is seen arriving at Ryde Esplanade with W32 *Bonchurch* in charge, the adjacent tramway being closed in 1969.

15 August 1964

Seventy-four-year-old 0-4-4T W14 *Fishbourne* arrives out of St Boniface Down into the amphitheatre Ventnor station existed in with the 13.27 from Ryde Pier Head. The station site is now an industrial park occupied by Southern Water, whose pipeline utilises the former railway tunnel.

22 August 1964
One of the few surviving Patriots, No. 45527 *Southport*, together with Stanier 4-6-0 No. 45339 are set to return happy holidaymakers to their North West homes. Initially named Hounds Hill, the appellation of Central was acquired in 1878. When Blackpool's other terminus, that of North, was recommended under the Beeching plan for closure, the local council, underscoring the fact that the Central station's site was of greater land value, opted to close it. Whilst most of the former station area is now covered by an amusement arcade and car park, the one-time approach tracks are now a road titled Seasiders Way.

24 August 1964
An overview of Leicester Midland shed from a road paralleling the shed with a pair of LMS 4Fs and a 9F, awaiting the next call for duty. Whilst the two elderly 0-6-0s didn't see the year's end, at least the young eight-year-old 9F escaped, upon the shed's closure to steam, to Birkenhead.

24 August 1964

Being one of the earliest public railways, and mainly intended for the transport of coal, the idea of carrying passengers had not occurred to the line's promoters. Facilities for purchasing tickets were provided as an afterthought at local inns or keepers of various road crossings. Such was the case at Leicester West Bridge until 1893, when, belatedly, a passenger station was constructed around 150 yards away, nearer to the houses on the (then new) Tudor Road.

24 August 1964

I was fortunate on the day of my visit because one of the two specially adapted BR 2MTs, No. 78013 (a cut-down cab roof to negotiate the height-restricted Glenfield tunnel), was shunting some coal wagons. Richard III Road now obscures the site.

25 August 1964
At the derelict-looking Derby Friargate station, Ivatt Mogul No. 43156 waits departure time
with the 13.00 for Nottingham Victoria. This train, formed of non-corridor stock, was to take
me along the remaining 18-mile truncated stub of the GNR's Derbyshire and Staffordshire
extension, part of which crossed the Erewash valley on the impressive 1,452-ft-long Bennerley
viaduct. Today little remains of the station except the bridge over Friargate itself, although the
remaining arches attached to the south side of the bridge on the right side reveal a boarded-up
arch, the inside of which contains the original staircase to the central island platforms.

and Livery Street before Snow Hill was settled upon in 1858. Starting off as a
nondescript wooden construction, a major revamp in 1871 equipped the station with
a glazed overall roof together with two through roads and two north end bays. The
prohibitive cost of widening the 635-yard-long tunnel at the south end of the station
resulted in Moor Street being born, in 1909, to deal with the burgeoning suburban
traffic from Leamington and Stratford. Further expansion a few years later, in order
to compete with the LMS's New Street services, saw the track-work north of the site
quadruple – together with a major upgrade to the station I was witnessing that August
visit. You could see that at one time, not so long ago, it was the jewel in the crown
of GWR, catering for expresses to/from all parts of the country. With its wide (once
carpeted as a marketing gimmick by Cyril Lord) staircases leading to the two major
platforms, this once great cathedral of steam was now suffering from an overdose
of fumes from DMUs that were ticking over. It was a hot and sunny day and in the
somewhat claustrophobic effect created by the tunnels at both ends it made for a sweaty,
uncomfortable visit – the aforementioned odours not helping. The one resident Pannier
tank, busying itself shunting parcel vans at the north end of the station (reputedly
the best position for trainspotting and photographing), together with an elderly tank
passing through light engine just about made the stay marginally more tolerable. On
my visit, however, the station had an eerie, underused atmosphere about it.

26 August 1964
Rebuilt by Collett from the frames of Churchward's 2-6-2T Class 5115 Prairie No. 8109, the last survivor of the once ten-strong class passes through the cavernous Birmingham Snow Hill station.

4 September 1965
Just over a year later Oxley-allocated No. 6833 *Calcot Grange*, shorn of number and nameplates, heads south through the station. In March '67, upon cessation of the Paddington to Birkenhead expresses, Snow Hill station went into a steep decline. All suburban services to the south were diverted from Moor Street and trains from Stourbridge and Shrewsbury were diverted to New Street, leaving just a handful of local stopping services from Wolverhampton Low Level. These were predictably withdrawn in 1972 and the station closed – the site was razed to the ground some five years later. With the saying what goes round comes around in mind, in 1987, with the local roads gridlocked, it was resurrected, albeit initially as a two-platformed concrete structure, as part of the Midland Metro – the full circle being completed some years later when the Marylebone to Kidderminster services were implemented.

I returned to my base that day via Shrewsbury, Crewe and Burton-on-Trent, travelling over the Coalville line – set to lose its passenger services the following month.

After one further local day spent visiting the GC line, in an attempt to photograph the famed windcutters, together with a visit to Leicester's Belgrave Road station, I headed home on the Saturday, calling in on the Newport Pagnell and Buckingham branches just for good measure – both lines closed within weeks.

September saw me head to Worcestershire for a trip over the Bromyard branch (with just days to spare!) – the abysmal service on offer forcing me to take a valuable day's leave. Having returned to Worcester itself, I alighted at the Foregate Street station in order to journey west to Hereford in yet another vexatious DMU. At last matters improved with both Hereford and the 22-mile line via Ross-on-Wye awash with steam. Opened in 1855 and converted from broad gauge fourteen years later, the northern section of this delightfully rural and scenic railway required extensive engineering to cross the meanders of the River Wye on no less than four occasions, with either embankments or short tunnels of necessity at each one.

26 August 1964
Situated in the fork of the Stafford and Shrewsbury lines south of the station, the twenty-minute walk to Crewe South shed was never undertaken. This vista was granted by hanging out of the train window during the customary signal stop outside Crewe station. I had never before seen such a large shed. Over the following three years, having headed north out of London, when approaching Crewe, often during the hours of darkness, upon seeing the welcoming sight of so many steam locomotives surrounded by the seemingly permanent sulphuric haze reflected in the yard lights, I knew, as a steam chaser, in my heart that whatever the weekend held, I was in the right part of the country. Regrettably, upon its closure to steam in November '67, rows of derelict, rusting hulks awaiting their fate were a more common sight.

27 August 1964
The GNR's Leicester Belgrave Road station had last seen regular passenger trains as far back as 1953. It was kept open for holidaymaker summer Saturday, and excursion traffic to the East Coast resorts of Skegness and Mablethorpe, but they too had ceased in September '62.

29 August 1964
Ebbw Junction's six-year-old 9F No. 92235, presumably having worked in over the long since deceased line via Verney Junction from Oxford, rests on Bletchley shed (1E).

29 August 1964

With passenger services ceasing the following month, this was yet another line built into my complex itinerary. Derby-built fifty-two-seat single railcar No. M79990, forming the 14.45 departure out of Buckingham for Bletchley, awaits its non-existent passengers. The station buildings have been completely demolished, leaving only the platform edges in a dilapidated state. The track bed through Buckingham, in filled to platform level, has become a wooded walk.

3 September 1964

Standing forlorn outside Worcester shed, withdrawn Castle 4-6-0 No. 5096 *Bridgewater Castle* awaits being towed to the breaker's yard. The shed closed to steam in December 1965.

3 September 1964
Hereford's 4-6-0
No. 6985 *Parwick Hall*
waits the signal to head
home – the signal box/
junction at Rotherwas
Junction closing with
the cessation of services
over the Ross line that
November.

Climbing on through Ross-on-Wye, the line peaked in the 771-yard-long Lea Line tunnel before descending through the Forest of Dean. However, scenery doesn't make for profitability – in two months' time the line was to lose its passenger trains, freight over the southern section lingering on into the following year.

Gloucester Central was another revelation – steam seemingly everywhere. Unable to encompass a trip on the Chalford auto, at least I took a photograph of one. That was just a foretaste of what was to be the biggest surprise of the outing. Notes have long been lost from that day but having selected the 18.15 departure for Swindon as a means to return to London, I cannot recall what brought the train from its starting station of Cheltenham, but I well remember the exhilaration at what took over. One of the last dozen or so Castles, 7005 *Sir Edward Elgar*, was to take me the 36¾ miles through Stroud and the Golden Valley that evening.

3 September 1964
Twenty-eight-year-old
0-6-0 No. 2287, at
Ross on Wye, crosses
the train I was on with
a northbound freight.
Heavy parcels traffic
seen on the platform
failed to save the line.
The station building
has been demolished
and the site redeveloped
into an industrial estate,
although the brick
goods and engine sheds
still stand.

3 September 1964
Despite widespread dieselisation elsewhere, this route was allowed to continue with steam, with no attempt to save money or offer a better service. My train, the 16.30 Hereford to Gloucester Central, waits time at Longhope, where I took the opportunity of the lengthy station stop, awaiting an opposite way working over the single line to photograph the train locomotive, Collett 5101 Class 2-6-2T No. 4161.

3 September 1964
One of the famed Golden Valley auto trains, the 17.15 from Chalford, is seen after arrival into Gloucester Central with Horton Road's 0-4-2T No. 1444. Beeching cuts saw to the ending of this service that November.

October saw me make a serious inroad into an attempt to travel with as many different SR-allocated steam locomotives as possible, by commencing twice weekly evening outings to Woking. Initially travelling out on the 17.09 Basingstoke commuter train, and returning on an 18.26 arrival into Waterloo from Bournemouth if a 'required' (i.e. never travelled with before locomotive) was on the 18.54 departure, I returned to Woking, finally finishing on either the 20.26 or 20.34 arrival back into Waterloo. This addiction to catching runs with as many steam locomotives as possible was to manifest itself on the Reading/Guildford/Redhill line during the final weeks of steam operation that year. Basing myself at Guildford and jumping on trains to/from their first stops of either Shalford or Wanborough, I was to redline twenty-nine steam locomotives from seven classes in my ever-present *Locoshed* Book, before dieselisation on the first Monday of '65.

Aware of wide-scale closures in North and Mid Wales, a twenty-four-hour, 600-mile (114 miles of which was to close within weeks) outing was undertaken that November. Having departed out of Euston, changing at Crewe, we caught the 02.19 Holyhead train which, although allegedly booked for a Britannia, was disappointingly worked by an English Electric Type 3, nicknamed 'Long Pongs'

31 October 1964
Guildford shed, seemingly carved out of a chalk cliff, is now the obligatory, albeit multi-storey, car park. First up is Q1 No. 33015, one of forty constructed during 1942. Classified as 5Fs, these 0-6-0s were built, taking into consideration the priority for metal at the front line, with the minimum of ornamentation. Nicknamed 'Coffee Pots', they were only called upon to work passenger trains upon failures or shortages within locomotive availability. I caught runs with two of them to/from Redhill that December.

31 October 1964
Now preserved at the Bluebell Railway, USA 0-6-0T No. 30064, the shed pilot and last locomotive to leave the shed in July '67, waits her call to duty.

(for obvious reasons) by us steam diehards, to Bangor. There, in the inky darkness of a November morning we travelled over a line just weeks before its closure on the 05.20 for Pwhelli – the only daily steam train on the Carnarvon line, all others being DMUs. Dawn had just about broken upon arrival into Pwhelli and with one of the group being a bus fanatic, the Crosville garage had to be visited before continuing our journey. After taking an all-stations stopper along the picturesque coast-clinging line to Barmouth, a 45-mile ride through the beautiful Welsh panorama via Llangollen to Ruabon was made. We were indeed fortunate because severe flooding the following month meant sections of this line were never to reopen prior to its closure that January. Then, making our way the short distance to the former Cambrian HQ of Oswestry, rather than wait in the dismal cold conditions a fill-in trip to/from Welshpool was made – alighting at Llanmynech for a journey over the Llanfyllin branch. Having then returned south via Whitchuch and Crewe, the never to be repeated travels were neatly entered into my books at home the following day.

14 November 1964
Ivatt Mogul No. 46521 arrives into Barmouth with the stock to form the 09.45 to Dolgellau. She was more fortunate than the line she was to traverse that day (closed the following January), in that she has survived into preservation at the Great Central Railway. No trace of Dolgellau station remains, having been buried beneath the A470 bypass.

14 November 1964

Shrewsbury's Ivatt No. 46512 is on that day's Llanfyllin branch duties and is seen after arrival at Oswestry with the 13.30 from Llanfyllin itself. Having worked that branch's last day's services in January '65, she was dispatched to Crewe South, where she was withdrawn in November '66. After spending several years at Barry, she is now preserved at the Strathspey Railway. The Grade II listed station building, once HQ of the Cambrian Railways, survives today. A heritage railway has plans to reopen the line to Gobowen.

14 November 1964

Shrewsbury's No. 7812 *Erlestoke Manor* departs Llanymynech with the 12.35 Aberystwyth to Whitchurch. The third fortunate survivor from that day's travels, it nowadays resides at the Severn Valley Railway. The former station site is now a heavy goods vehicle car park.

1965

That year started off pretty quietly from a railway-travelling point of view – the long cold days not conducive to hanging around waiting for trains. On the final Friday of February, bearing in mind the Cuckoo line trains out of Eastbourne were being truncated at Tunbridge Wells West from the following Monday, I shuttled between Tonbridge and Eridge, collecting runs with the six BR Standard 4MT tanks in circulation. This closure by stealth scenario (i.e. deterring prospective through passengers) was one of many methods employed by BR back then in order to justify eventual closure on the basis of poor patronage.

On three Saturdays that spring, aware of the WR's hell-bent intention to rid itself of steam by the year's end, I caught the northbound 'Pines Express' from Basingstoke to Banbury, returning on the southbound York to Bournemouth. It was the latter

February 1965
The lunchtime arrival of the milk empties from Vauxhall are seen in the front of the 300+ lever all-electric signal box. As the office 'gopher' there were several occasions that permitted me to visit it. The site has subsequently been obliterated by Waterloo International station.

train which had attracted my attention – the 22¾-mile portion between Banbury and Oxford being one of the few remaining all-year passenger services worked by the fast dwindling number of GWR-built (predominantly from the Hall or Grange classes) locomotives. A variation to the above was made one day in May by travelling on the northbound to York, which, after the GW steam power had relinquished the train at Banbury to a Type 3 DL, then traversed the former Great Central line to Nottingham Victoria. I returned to the 'smoke' that day on a train I was to frequent on a great number of occasions, prior to the line's closure in September '66; the 17.15 semi Nottingham Victoria to Marylebone. This was the third of the three daily trains over the line, which had essentially been left to die by BR – its irregular timetabled trains formed of sub-standard coaching stock with dereliction and decay visible all along the line no doubt deterring any prospective punters.

Later that month I returned to the Cuckoo line to travel over its entirety, prior to its closure that June. I accessed it by travelling over the Three Bridges to Groombridge, via the East Grinstead (High Level) line. Also closing on the same date was the Guildford to Horsham line. Deliberately homing in on the evening rush hour Cranleigh-terminating service, the rumoured usage of a Guilford Q1 was disappointingly thwarted. The timetable changes that summer also heralded the dieselisation of the

11 May 1965
This idyllic country station setting at Hellingly sees Redhill's No. 80141 arriving with the 15.14 Tunbridge Wells West to Eastbourne service. There was also a separate platform for passengers visiting a nearby asylum, an associated electric tramway being principally constructed for the conveyance of coal to the hospital's boiler house. Closed to passengers in 1931, the branch survived until 1959 when the boilers were converted to oil. The station building survives today as a private residence, complete with canopy. The track bed has been converted to the Cuckoo Trail public footpath and cycleway.

19 May 1965

Three weeks away from closure, sister Mickey No. 41294 arrives into Cranleigh with the 18.34 rush-hour terminating extra from Guildford. The station buildings were demolished shortly afterwards, being replaced by a housing and shopping development. In 2004 part of this development was itself demolished and a Sainsbury supermarket was built on the site. The station's original platforms still exist behind the shops – the track bed being part of the 37-mile Downs Link footpath between St Martha's Hill (Guildford) and Shoreham-by-Sea.

19 May 1965

Mickey No. 41287 waits time at Baynards with the 18.15 Horsham to Guildford. The station was built for the Liberal politician Lord Thurlow, the owner of nearby Baynards Park, whose land was on the route of the proposed railway line. As a condition of sale, Lord Thurlow insisted on having a station built to serve his estate, despite there being no nearby settlement. Now fully restored as a private residence, the majority of the line forms part of the Downs Link footpath.

19 May 1965
Taken just a month prior to closure, the evening rush hour services cross at Baynards. The 18.05 Guildford to Horsham had Ivatt No. 41299 in charge.

19 May 1965
The driver of our train, the 18.15 ex-Horsham, hands the single line token over to the Peasmarsh Junction signalman before then heading into Guildford along the Portsmouth to London main line.

Cardiff to Portsmouth via Salisbury, Romsey and Southampton trains, and so a visit to them was made, with the Portsmouth portion of the daily Plymouth to Brighton train in the mix – all being worked by variations of BR Standard types.

The last week of that May saw me make my first visit to Scotland. I was primarily lured by the imminent closure of the Port Road (Dumfries/Stranraer), and favourable reports of the LNER A4's performances on the three-hour expresses between Aberdeen and Glasgow. Regrettably, with travel costs being prioritised over the associated production costs of photographs, although the terminus of Edinburgh Princes Street and Glasgow St Enoch were visited, no pictorial record of them was taken.

Back in the south, in June I travelled the 67½ miles to Banbury out of Paddington on the 16.15 stopper – a week before it became the final booked steam departure out of Brunel's terminus. My steed for the outing was an unnumbered, nameless, externally unkempt 6952 *Kimberley Hall*; it was a stark contrast to the bulled-up *Clun Castle* a week later.

After a two-week family holiday to the Italian Riviera, followed by an overnight (via Salisbury, Templecombe and Poole) trip to Weymouth in order to travel from the Dorset resort to Oxford through the steam-starved WR route, via Yeovil and Swindon to Oxford, I once again headed for Scotland. Although suffering nearly six hours of that day in DMUs, predominantly in order to travel over the doomed Fife Coast line via Crail, at least a more than compensatory visit to Glasgow's Buchanan Street station with A4 *Sir Nigel Gresley*, followed by the return overnight to London having *Clan Macleod* on it as far as Carstairs, somewhat made up for it. This overnight train was routed, because of ongoing WCML electrification work south of Rugby, from Northampton, via Blisworth, Bletchley, Claydon LNE Junction and Calvert into Marylebone.

29 May 1965
'The Northern Irishman', having completed its 406-mile, ten-hour journey from London, is seen at Stranraer Harbour at 05.30 hours, two weeks before the Port Road closed, causing the train to be rerouted an extra 43 miles, via Maunchline and Ayr.

11 July 1965
Whilst waiting for the start-up of services over the S&D, I bunked Templecombe shed. Wandering around (unchallenged), an air of neglect and abandonment seemed to prevail – the silent locomotives dripping with early morning mist (it was 05.15, after all!).

24 July 1965
Taken from my St Andrews-bound DMU train, Thompson-designed B1 No. 61148 is seen propelling the stock into Thornton Junction station to form the 12.03 for Crail. With the closure of the remaining stub of the Fife Coast Railway (that to Leven) four years later, Thornton Junction's purpose was deemed surplus. This seemingly short-sighted decision was undermined with the creation of the Glenrothes-with-Thornton station, which was opened in 1992.

24 July 1965
Another shot taken by leaning out of my DMU train sees sister B1 No. 61102 arriving into Anstruther with the 12.30 summer Saturdays only Crail to Edinburgh Waverley. Not having had a run with an example of that class, I returned two weeks later, deliberately homing in on this train, albeit just for the short distance over the Forth Bridge into Edinburgh.

24 July 1965

This is Glasgow Buchanan Street, at which I had arrived behind A4 No. 60007 *Sir Nigel Gresley*, working that day's Grampian, the 13.30 from Aberdeen. Opened in 1849 as the Caledonian Railway's main terminus for the city, the original two platforms were doubled in 1932 by the LMS. Never provided with an overall roof, the platforms were covered with redundant awnings from Ardrossan North. In comparison to all the other Glasgow termini, the station had a wearisome tiredness about it.

24 July 1965

The simultaneously timed (17.30) *St Mungo* departed with A4 No. 60024 *Kingfisher*. The offices of Buchanan House, together with the Glasgow Caledonian University, **now** occupy the site of the station.

13 August 1965
Feltham motive power depot, situated within the 32 miles of marshalling yard tracks and targeted by the Luftwaffe in the Second World War, was the final home for the Urie S15 Class. No. 30833, having been withdrawn that May, was seen minus her coupling rods.

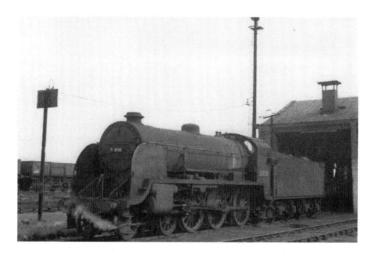

13 August 1965
Sister No. 30838 is seen in light steam, her end coming with the class cull the following month. A maintenance depot is currently (2020) being constructed on the site to house new-build EMUs.

I was also homing in on the afternoon semis out of Marylebone, these being a consistent source of Stanier Black 5s from a variety of sheds throughout the LMR. Twice however, just for a change, my route to them called for a variation. On the first occasion I accessed them via Richmond and Broad Street – the other after bunking Feltham shed, the final refuge of the S15s, having been evicted out of Southall shed.

Two further visits to Scotland were made that August and, after thwarted (by seriously late running Anglo-Scottish overnight trains) attempts at reaching Aberdeen behind steam, at least I was able to travel over the Tayport branch (1879–1969) and the Alloa to Larbert line over the Throsk swing bridge, together with further runs with A4s and another Clan. Indeed, as my hobby was now morphing into steam chasing rather than track bashing, runs with LNER B1s and an A2, together with a Jubilee, didn't disappoint.

With the dying days of that summer, the Saturday wavy-lined trains over the Oxford, Birmingham Snow Hill and Wolverhampton Low Level lines were targeted

13 August 1965

I was not so lucky at attempting to bunk Southall shed later that day, being told to 'clear orf out of here', or words to that effect, by the ever-vigilant foreman. Having already noted the preserved Castle No. 4079 *Pendennis Castle* in residence, I snatched this shot of a 61XX on the way out.

21 August 1965

Although not in the Beeching report, closure notices of the line from Alloa to Larbert had been published. Extensive repairs to the Throsk swing bridge over the River Forth were considered financially unviable. A pair of J37s are at rest on Alloa shed. Reopened from Stirling, in 2008, sufficient patronage led to it being electrified in 2018.

28 August 1965

A hurriedly taken shot (from a departing northbound train) of Oxford shed. The dilapidated wooden shed, looking as if it's about to fall apart, is of West Midland Railway (1862) origin, with one of its three Panniers, No. 9789, to survive until the end.

4 September 1965
Creeping past the
remains of the
former GWR station,
originally built to
the broad-gauge
dimension, en
route home is
4-6-0 No. 6991 *Acton
Burnall Hall*. She was
withdrawn at the year's
end in the WR cull.

4 September 1965
One of Oxley's
handful of Britannias,
No. 70053 *Moray
Firth* (drafted in to
replace of the Castles
on the West of England
summer Saturday
services) arrives into
Wolverhampton Low
Level with the 11.10
from Ilfracombe.

as they were the most likely source of trains powered by former GWR locomotives.
Several Saturdays running, some of them having fulfilled my obligatory Saturday
morning duties at my Waterloo office, I intercepted them at either Basingstoke
or Reading, changing en route to Wolverhampton as requirements dictated.
With the last of those occasions allowing a two-hour sojourn at Banbury, a most
photographically rewarding visit was made to the shed there.

September, and I took what I thought was my final visit to the S&D – closure notices
having been posted. The steamiest way west was to catch the 22.35 Weymouth-bound
TPO out of Waterloo, changing at Eastleigh onto a 02.02 Bristol train. With
the S&D services yet to start up, I filled in the early hours of that morning with
a trip over the Severn Beach branch. Fortunately avoiding the Hymeck-powered
Bath services out of Temple Meads, upon arrival into Bath, sufficient time allowed
a shed bash before heading south over the 'new' main line to Templecombe. What
a memorable journey that was (fully detailed in my 2013 book *The Great Steam
Chase*), the Standard 5MT vociferously ploughing her way over the Mendips.

Above: 4 September 1965
Another arrival from the south
that evening had Standard
5MT No. 73036 in charge. In
this scene you can see the close
proximity of the High Level
station in the background.
Although closed to passengers in
1972, for many years afterwards
the station was used as a Parcel
Concentration Depot. The
Grade II listed main building
subsequently found a new lease
of life as a banqueting hall and
wedding venue.

Right: 11 September 1965
The opportunity, due to
an hour connectional wait
between trains, presented itself
to bunk Banbury shed and,
being situated to the south
of the station on the west
side of the line, it was just an
easy ten-minute walk. What a
feast of steam was to be seen.
First up is Willesden-allocated
2-8-0 Stanier 8F No. 48010 at
rest. She was to end her days at
Newton Heath in January '68.

Gloucester-allocated Fowler-designed Armstrong Whitworth-built forty-three-year-old 4F No. 44560 reposes in the sun – this former S&D locomotive had been withdrawn just days earlier.

This 1942 North British-built 2-8-0, No. 48220, is raring to go home. Perhaps to Saltley depot?

Once working the famed GC Windcutters when allocated at Annesley, this now Banbury resident BR 9F No. 92074 is under the coal chute.

Here we see visiting Machynlleth-allocated BR 4MT No. 75004. I was to view her again in her own territory working a freight the following month. I finally caught a run with her in September '66, along the Welsh Marches line.

This Banbury shed scene sees resident 0-6-2T No. 6697, an engine that was to be transferred to Croes Newydd by the end of the year (a move that ensured its survival as one of the last two members of its class), and a surprising visitor in the form of BoB No. 34051 *Winston Churchill*. Both locomotives survived into preservation, albeit as static displays.

A very healthy steam scene featuring Nos 75004, 48010, 45052, 6934 *Beachamwell Hall* and No. 48220 in the line-up. Whilst the WR rid itself of steam by the year's end, Banbury remained open until the October of '66. This was necessary to deal with visitors off the SR, together with the ex-GC requirements.

18 September 1965
BR 3MT No. 82041 appears dwarfed within the fading grandeur of the former Midland
Railway terminus as she sits on the stock which was to form the 10.10 Bristol Temple Meads
departure. The station has become a Grade II listed building, the former booking hall is now the
Green Park Brasserie. The old station concourse is used as a covered market and events space,
with local events and performances scheduled throughout the year.

18 September 1965
With no one around, I accessed this shed by walking off the end of the platform and along the
trackside. I came across the locomotive destined to take me across the Mendips that day: BR
Standard 4-6-0 No. 73068.

18 September 1965

Twenty-five-year-old 0-6-0PT No. 3659 rests outside Bath Green Park shed. On paper she was allocated to Templecombe but, presumably never returning home, she was withdrawn here the following month.

18 September 1965

Busying herself on the same day, sister No. 3758, whose career history had included lengthy stays at both Bristol sheds of St Philips Marsh and Barrow Road, is seen near her home depot of Bath Green Park.

18 September 1965

BR 4MT No. 80039 leads the 09.00 Bristol Temple Meads to Branksome down the incline from Templecombe (Upper) to the S&D line.

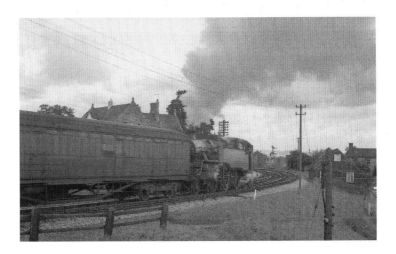

18 September 1965
The one-time axis of the S&D, this station acquired its junction status upon the opening, in 1874, of the line to Bath and was noted for the wonderful display of hanging baskets overflowing with flowers. The traditional viewpoint of northbound departing trains from Evercreech Junction was utilised in this shot of BR Standard 4MT No. 75072 powering away with the 11.41 Bournemouth Central to Bristol Temple Meads.

18 September 1965
I had alighted there to catch the one-coach, one-van 13.15 departure along the former 'main line' to Highbridge, worked that day by Mickey No. 41223.

18 September 1965
Having alighted off an incoming train just minutes earlier I ran, hell for leather, back along the track to capture Ivatt No. 41307 storming away from Highbridge with the 14.18 Templecombe departure. The Burnham extension was closed to regular passenger traffic in 1951, the occasional special continuing to use it until 1962. There is no trace of the former S&DJR platforms, engine shed or works, all of which are now beneath a new housing estate.

In comparison, I then took a sedate ride over the Somerset Levels to Highbridge before calling in at Chippenham for a ride over the Calne branch on its last day of operation.

Over the years I made three visits to the Isle of Wight railway system and, upon learning of the proposed demise of the Cowes and Ventnor tentacles, revisited them, camera in hand. Suitably equipped with a line side permit, inexperience, poor positioning (call it what you like) led to a selection of shots, mostly mediocre, and not publishable within this book.

Now mid-October and, after an overnight trip to sample the last days of the Manors over the Cambrian line from Shrewsbury to Aberystwyth, I headed north, via Chester, to Birkenhead Woodside station. As dusk had fallen it wasn't until further visits the following year that I could appreciate the neglect and abandonment that pervaded this once grandiose terminal. I then made my way to Manchester Central to board the 22.50 two-coach, one-van train for the overnight run to Marylebone, via Guide Bridge, Sheffield Victoria and Leicester Central. I enjoyed this journey so much (with its four traction changes en route: steam/DC EL, DL, steam and DL, in that order) that I was to ensure future visits to the north funnelled me onto this train on a further five occasions before its cessation in September '66.

Most of the rest of that year was spent on SR metals, attempting to obtain runs with all the remaining Bulleid Pacifics. Keeping an eye out for variations off the main Bournemouth line, on one occasion I called in at the Southampton terminus,

21 September 1965
Having just departed Wroxall, Adams O2 No. W28 *Ashey* is about to enter the 1,312-yard-long tunnel to Ventnor whilst working the 13.27 Ryde Pier Head to Ventnor. The station has since been demolished, with a new road running across the south end of the site. The adjacent Station Hotel has been converted into residential units.

21 September 1965
An overview of No. W27 *Merstone* taken from the station footbridge at Newport later that same day. It is preparing to work the 17.05 SX rush hour extra for Ryde St Johns Road. Once the junction of four different routes, no trace of the site exists today. The nearby section of the island's only dual carriageway caters for present-day commuters.

21 September 1965

Highlighting the unique self-release shunting arrangement that operated at Cowes, No. W26 *Whitwell* is seen propelling the stock up the 1 in 95 incline, having worked in on the 17.18 from Ryde Pier Head. Despite there being a crossover at the terminal end between the two main platforms, the trains were often too long to allow the incoming locomotive to take immediate advantage of it. Instead, once clear of passengers, the train would be propelled back a little and hand-braked, the locomotive then running forward to use the crossover and parallel platform line. The stock would then be allowed to run down the gradient under control of the guard, so that, once at rest and braked, the locomotive could complete its running around and be coupled on the Newport end.

16 October 1965

I certainly needed the guidance from Lt Aiden Fuller's *Shed Directory* for this visit to Shrewsbury shed, it being a twenty-five-minute walk through unfamiliar streets. First up is Croes Newydd-allocated 2-8-0 No. 3855, withdrawn two months earlier and awaiting the call of the cutter's torch. She was, however, one of the fourteen locomotives seen on my visit to Shrewsbury shed that survived into preservation. Having spent twenty-two years at Barry, she is now at the East Lancashire Railway.

With little revenue-earning usage for a 2MT locomotive, Croes Newydd's 2-6-2T No. 84000 (with sacking over its chimney to stop birds nesting) lies dead at the back of Shrewsbury shed.

Displaced from her lifelong (twelve years) residency at Oswestry, upon that shed's closure to steam in January '65, Swindon-built Ivatt 2MT No. 46511 rusts away on 6D.

Lifelong Shrewsbury resident nineteen-year-old 0-6-0PT No. 9657 is in light steam. Visiting Croes Newydd 2-8-0 8F No. 48440 lurks in the background.

Shrewsbury shed hosts Oxford's No. 6947 *Helmingham Hall*, named after a moated Suffolk manor, once used as a location for the BBC's *Antiques Roadshow*. I had a run with her between Oxford and Banbury the previous March whilst en route from Basingstoke to Nottingham on the once a day Bournemouth to Newcastle train.

Fresh from her exertions on that morning's 'Cambrian Coast Express', twenty-seven-year-old Collett-designed 4-6-0, the subsequently preserved No. 7802 *Bradley Manor*, takes a well-earned rest.

and two others, on the same Sunday. Resulting from engineering works was the freight-only West Byfleet to Addlestone curve, and the Wimbledon to Wandsworth Town, via East Putney LT line – the latter normally the preserve of empty stock trains. Finally, I just had to make one last visit to Oxford whilst the remnants of GWR power still existed. With all the WR steam stock (excepting the S&D) being condemned on 3 January '66, what was left was indeed a sight for sore eyes.

28 December 1965
My final photograph of an active WR-allocated steam locomotive. Thirty-four-year-old No. 6111 was in the yard adjacent to Oxford station – formally the LNWR terminus of Rewley Street. The station building components were moved to the Buckinghamshire Railway Centre, where they were refurbished and re-erected as a visitor centre and display building, which formally opened in 2002.

11 November 1965
An earlier view of the yard (in the background) can be seen in this view of a rundown No. 6953 *Leighton Hall* passing through Oxford station with a lightweight freight. Once hauling prestige passenger trains, the neglect and uncared-for external condition, with her name and number plates missing, was how the WR authorities, having not filled engine cleaner vacancies for some time, treated a once fine example of British workmanship.

1966

With the early part of the year spent obtaining the maximum possible steam train mileages, utilising my London to Southampton season ticket, which included travelling on the prestigious all-Pullman 'Bournemouth Belle' together with the overnight mail and newspaper trains, I had a sudden realisation of a line closure right under my nose that meant taking an emergency day's leave on Friday 11 February for the Fawley line's last day of operation.

Two weeks later and one final visit to the S&D had to be made. Similar to the sulky service run over the East Grinstead to Lewes line ten years earlier, the WR had a local bus company pulling out of the supposedly agreed road replacement

7 February 1966
Nine Elms Standard 3MT No. 82018 departs Clapham Junction with the 08.16 (unadvertised Post Office) train for Kensington Olympia. The signal box the train is about to pass under, Clapham Junction 'A', had a steel roof put over it during the Second World War, the 40-ton weight of which contributed to its subsidence in May '65. It was removed after this.

11 February 1966
The twice-daily DEMU service over the Fawley branch ceased on the second Friday in the February of '66. This first scene shows the 15.46 from Eastleigh after its arrival at Fawley.

The station sign.

This outing was my first – last – train. A series of detonators were later placed at the 1961-built Frost Lane Crossing signal box. Whilst the inwards train was packed, the returning 16.48 departure, was full and standing. After alighting at the junction station of Totton, a visit to the ticket office produced some SR examples: sold after the final train had gone!

9 April 1967
I returned to Fawley once more, courtesy of the unusual usage of two examples of the 0-6-0T USA tanks (whose normal duties were within Southampton Docks), whilst on the Hampshire Branch Lines Railtour. Several attempts have been made (to date without success) to reopen the branch: the latest proposal, funding permitted, is a half-hourly service from Southampton.

26 February 1966
Ivatt No. 41296 stands out of use at Templecombe, her services never wanted again. The shed was adjacent to the low-level platform on the S&D line but was easily accessed from the upper level with a five-minute walk. Everything bar the signal box was demolished following closure a week later. The station was reopened in 1983 following the local council and residents' support and has seen a year on year increase in passenger usage.

26 February 1966
On the penultimate Saturday, Bournemouth's BR Mogul No. 76011 slakes her thirst whilst working the 06.00 Bristol Temple Meads to Branksome. The residual station buildings are now private homes. The nearby public house, nowadays the Natterjack Inn, was, for a few years following the line's closure, appropriately named the Silent Whistle.

26 February 1966

With just one week to go before the postponed closure of the S&D, just one more trip had to be made. The disgraceful 'sulky' service, in which just a handful of trains were run at inconvenient un-connecting times, led us to catch the only through southbound train of the day: the 06.00 Bristol Temple Meads to Branksome. It was a bitterly cold day and the few photographs taken were from when briefly opening the window, whilst enjoying the saturating warmth of a steam-heated compartment.

26 February 1966

Eulogised in Flanders and Swann's 'Slow Train', my thoughts were with signalmen possibly contemplating redundancy or a move to a power box. Since 1995, a preservation group has taken over the station and operates trains over a small section of track.

26 February 1966
The only
northbound train
of the morning, the
07.00 Templecombe
to Bath Green
Park, is crossed
at Shepton Mallet
(Charlton Road) with
BR Standard 4MT
No. 80043 in charge.

services at the last minute, imposing an appalling stopgap service over the route. We travelled on the 06.00 Bristol Temple Meads to Branksome – the only daily through southbound service, which took 4½ hours for the 82-mile journey. After witnessing the sights of dereliction and decay following years of calculated neglect and (financial) starvation, the end, a week later, couldn't come quick enough.

Promotion within the clerical grades of BR took me to the South Eastern Division of the former Southern Region and, in a bid to familiarise myself with various station and siding layouts, a day out with a Train Inspector included a visit to Ashford Works, camera in hand.

3 March 1966
The first of three very fortunate locomotives, in that they all survived into preservation, No. DS237 *Maunsell*, is seen at Ashford Works. Together with sister USA *Wainwright*, they reside at the K&ESR.

3 March 1966

0-6-0T No. DS238 *Wainwright* (formerly No. 30070), another transfer in from Southampton Docks, is also seen at work during my visit. Both USAs were withdrawn in September '67.

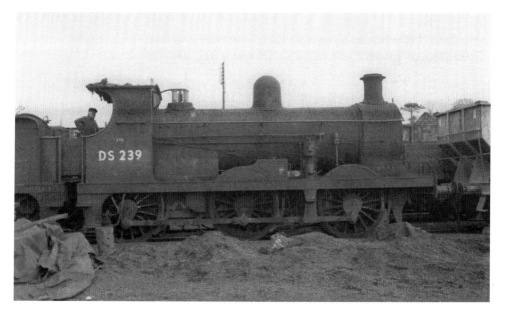

3 March 1966

1902 Longhedge-built C 0-6-0 No. DS239 (formerly No. 31592) was withdrawn at the end of 1966, destined for a lifetime of preservation at the Bluebell Railway.

Another month, another closure. This time it was the Adur valley line from Shoreham-by-sea to Christ's Hospital, via Steyning. On its last day of service, a group of us peeled away from the Bournemouth steam services at Southampton Central and made our way over to the Sussex line.

Unsure of where I was going with my railway career, I attended a rules and signalling class held at Clapham Junction. Why not? I thought. Every Tuesday evening, I would travel from my Cannon Street office, via Kensington, and commute on the Post Office 'Kenny Belle'. Football meetings often warranted extras back then. To this effect,

6 March 1966
It was the Adur valley line's last day of running and, at the stations that still had manned ticket offices (it was a Sunday after all!), some of us held the door of the DEMU open whilst others dashed to the booking office to purchase souvenir (some of them of Southern Railway antiquity) tickets. Whilst Southwater station was demolished to make way for road improvements, the track bed now forms part of the Downs Link footpath.

6 March 1966
Years later I naively exchanged the tickets bought that day for either a Rolling Stones or Beatles LP.

12 March 1966
With promotion thoughts within the football league in mind, a Footex was run from Southampton to Wolverhampton, worked by a rather grubby Merchant Navy No. 35027 *Port Line*, seen here after arrival at Wolverhampton Low Level. She substituted for the a specially cleaned but failed *Clan Line*.

a wonderful penetration through the steam-starved WR to Wolverhampton was enjoyed behind a Merchant Navy locomotive that March. Whilst the fans went to the match, us steam enthusiasts took the opportunity to pop up to Gobowen, thus collecting a couple of rides with two Stanier 5MTs. Word had got around amongst our Midland colleagues and whilst there were a mere six enthusiasts on the outward journey, the numbers swelled to over twenty on the return!

In the April of '66 the full WCML electrification of Trent Valley line services was implemented. Spurred on by the fact that displaced DLs would massacre the steam-operated services north of Crewe, a four-night, five-day bash was undertaken two weeks prior. After an overnight journey to Whitehaven, I made the short trip north to Workington, the intention being to travel onwards via Maryport to Carlisle. Fortunately, after observing a closure notice on the platform, plans were swiftly altered to travel over the Cockermouth and Keswick line instead. After visiting (without a permit) both Carlisle sheds, I made my way over Ais Gill, entering into the steam-saturated West Riding – an area that, having witnessed many passenger trains still being operated by steam, I vowed to return to as soon as possible. After returning to LMR territory and hitting upon the WCML steam services, which were being dieselised at the following month's timetable changes, I made my way home on, you guessed it, the 22.50 Manchester Central to Marylebone.

31 March 1966
At Workington shed Ivatt Mogul No. 46432 waits her next turn of duty. Transferred to Springs Branch, Wigan, after 12D's closure, I was aboard a shunt move worked by her when she attached the Manchester portion onto the rear of the Liverpool to Scotland overnight sleeper train. All movements counted back in those days! The site is a car park nowadays.

31 March 1966
A twenty-minute walk took me to Carlisle's Upperby shed – the one-time home to Scots, Patriots and Duchesses for the WCML services. First up is former ER Brit No. 70001 *Lord Hurcomb*, named after the first chairman (1948–53) of the – then – newly created British Transport Commission.

Former WR, then Crewe North, allocated Brit No. 70019 *Lightening*, with her coupling rods no doubt recycled for use on a more active sister, awaits her move to the scrap yard.

Sister Brit No. 70029 *Shooting Star*, also a prime performer on services out of Paddington, has already been relieved of her nameplates. She was to take me over Shap at 03.00 six months later, prior to being reallocated to Kingmoor.

Above: Mickey Mouse Ivatt No. 41217 rests between duties. She had led a varied and nomadic life, being allocated at several Manchester area sheds, then Southport, before arriving here in February '65.

Right: Ivatt 2-6-0 No. 46513, once a long-term Oswestry resident but displaced here in June '65, awaits her next call to duty. With little work remaining for a 2MT, she was dispatched to the cutter's torch four months hence.

The increased income resulting from the aforementioned promotion now allowed me to participate on railtours – the first being the A4 Commemorative Railtour from Waterloo to Exeter and back, whilst the second was the Hants & Wilts Railtour. Whilst no lines threatened with closure were travelled over on that occasion, in April, the Longmoor Tour certainly made up for it with a trip around the Hollywater Loop thrown in the mix.

Having thoroughly enjoyed the earlier visit to NER metals, a return far lengthier was made that May. An expected steam train out of York failed to materialise and a compensatory unchallenged visit to York shed was undertaken. Later that day, having misread the timetable, an opportunity to view the seemingly continuous parade of WD 2-8-0s through the then train shed-roofed Wakefield Kirkgate was relished.

Then onto the Bradford stations of Forster Square and Exchange. For sure, steam only worked the 9 miles to Leeds or 17 miles to Wakefield, but beggars can't be choosers and I was grateful for what I got. Needless to say, I returned south after that bash on the overnight GC line train.

3 April 1966
Salisbury shed was visited on the day of the Wilts & Hants Railtour, following those more knowledgeable than I from the station. Deep in the shed I came across Standard Mogul No. 76007. This seemingly elusive (on passenger trains) locomotive was finally caught, courtesy of inside information at my Wimbledon office, on a Bournemouth to Woking stopper just two weeks before the end of SR steam in July '67.

Right: 3 April 1966
Seen being serviced at 70E, this Maunsell U, together with N No. 31411, were the railtour favourites during their last months of existence, them being in the best condition.

Below: 3 April 1966
Thirty-two-year-old N 2-6-0 No. 31411, withdrawn after her Longmoor tour duties two weeks hence, also receives some TLC whilst on shed.

16 April 1966
Longmoor Military Railway was visited that April, WD600 *Gordon* taking over from the two aforementioned Maunsell moguls at Woking and worked via Liss, Longmoor and Bordon to Staines. The tour was double-headed into the camp from Liss with 0-6-0ST WD195.

A run past with WD196 *Errol Lonsdale* on the Hollywater loop – a six-mile circular route within the camp on which the REME (army) practise every kind of engineering skill. The locomotive survived into preservation in Belgium.

WD 601
Kitchener, seen
at Longmoor
Downs
station – she
was destroyed
before the year's
end, having
been used as
a demolition
target.

13 May 1966

Resulting from an expected steam-worked passenger being hauled by a DL, we bunked York
Shed (50A). Here in these six photographs is a selection of steam locomotive types still extant
at the time of my visit. First up is the Peppercorn-designed A1 No. 60145 *Saint Mungo*. This
Darlington-built seventeen-year-old 8P had, during 1965, sporadically rescued a few trains on
the ECML due to DL failures and, in that year, had powered a special end of class outing to
Newcastle and back. Although she was in a line of dead locomotives, the official withdrawal
date was documented as being the following month.

A wonderful vista from a bygone age as four home-allocated locomotives from four different classes surround the turntable. From left to right we have: No. 92006, a 1954 Crewe-built Riddles-designed 2-10-0; then WD No. 90078 and B1 No. 61017 *Bushbuck* (both not seeing the year's end); and finally, fresh from station pilot duties, K1 No. 62028.

Drink in the atmosphere – Horwich-built *Flying Pig* No. 43123 is seen surrounded by the detritus of a working shed.

Then two B1 4-6-0s face-off inside the shed, No. 61238 *Leslie Runciman* being nearest the camera.

Between 1943 and 1946 a total of 733 of these Riddles-designed War Department 2-8-0s, nicknamed 'Dub-dees' (due to the horrendous racket the motion made), were built for use both here and in Northern Europe to get things going after the devastation of the Second World War. Here, twenty-two-year-old North British-built No. 90395 appears to be receiving works attention. She was subsequently transferred to Sunderland, being withdrawn there six months later.

Finally, the end looks near for seventeen-year-old K1 No. 62012 with her chimney covered with sacking. Despite appearances, she was to survive a further year, ending her days at Sunderland in May '67. Closed to steam just thirteen months later, the site is now occupied by the National Railway Museum.

13 May 1966

Having misread the timetable, we became stranded at Wakefield Kirkgate for an hour. It wasn't, however, boring with a seemingly continuous stream of WD-hauled freights passing through. 2-8-0 No. 90407 heads westwards with a lengthy load.

Then, sister No. 90642 is seen waiting for the signal for the shed. The station had an air of neglect about it, not helped by the many panes missing from the nearly overall roof. It was completely removed six years later, presumably for its perilous condition. Often in the news, in respect of vandalism and other antisocial activities, a royal visit by Prince Charles during 2012 kick-started a multi-million-pound improvement scheme that was completed in 2015.

14 May 1966

Bradford Exchange, being a relatively small terminal, to me epitomises the steam era, with locomotives often standing at buffer stops for lengthy periods. Their steam and smoke entrapped under the sooty, grimy train shed, the station simply oozed atmosphere. With LNER B1s, and LMS tanks and Moguls on the Leeds and Wakefield portions, and Black Fives and Jubilees on the summer Saturday trains to North Wales, Fylde coast and east coast resorts, what more could a steam chaser want? First, we have Low Moor-allocated B1 No. 61386, having brought in the portion detached at Wakefield Westgate off the 10.20 from King's Cross.

18 June 1966
Borrowed from Mirfield
perhaps? This Black 5MT
readies herself to work the
17 miles to Wakefield with
the 13.05 for King's Cross.

2 July 1966
Cheating a bit here! At
Bridlington Low Moor's pet,
Jubilee No. 45565 *Victoria*,
has arrived with the 08.20
from Bradford Exchange –
92 miles of sheer heaven.

22 April 1967
With two weeks to go
before the portions were
discontinued, a consequence
of Leeds Central's closure,
Fairburn 2-6-4T No. 42116
is about to work the 11.00
for King's Cross.

30 September 1967
The final Saturday of NER steam saw a flood of enthusiasts willingly cough up 3/6d to travel
the 9½ miles to Leeds on the 09.55 'Yorkshire Pullman' with MNA cleaned B1 No. 61306.
In 1973 the station was rebuilt 50 yards to the south and renamed Interchange because of the
adjacent bus station. The former site was razed to the ground.

That neatly brings me onto the line the train mentioned above traversed –
the ex-Great Central. What can one say about this line, the greatest loss to the
travelling public ever? Deliberately run down upon the regional boundary changes
in 1958, when the route was awarded to the LMR, when I chanced across the
line in the autumn of '64, all that remained were three semi-fasts, a couple of
rush-hour locals and an overnight. Over thirty visits were made to the line and
by changing at the intermediate stations of Aylesbury, Woodford Halse, Rugby
Central, Ashby Magna and Leicester Central I accumulated runs with over forty
different locomotives – predominantly Black 5MTs and Brits. How useful would
the line be nowadays with its wider than normal loading gauge and prevailing 1 in
176 gradients? With Britain's roads expected to be gridlocked by 2050 and (at the
time of writing) various HS2 route machinations being debated methinks Barbara
Castle, the Labour Transport Minister of the day, made an error of judgement in
agreeing its closure.

Oh, I nearly forgot. That May, based on grapevine rumours that LNER
2-6-0 Class K1s still worked the Alnwick shuttles, a couple of us headed there with
fingers crossed, on what was to turn out to be the final day of steam operation.
Right time, right place. I was not always so lucky but that was the scenario I would
too often encounter during those years.

***Above and below*: 13 June 1966**

Ashby Magna was one of the two local stations (the other being East Leake) escaping the 1963 closures along the former GCR and, having alighted off the 17.20 from Rugby, can be seen with the almost empty M1 in the background. When the station was staffed, I had to take refuge in the gent's urinal to avoid a ticket check, being unsure of the validity of my Weymouth to Perth free pass. Nearing the final days of the line, however, with no one around I was able to wander freely enough to take these shots. Today a timber merchant occupies the site.

13 June 1966

The 17.20 SX starter for Nottingham Victoria is waiting to be platformed at Rugby Central after the 14.38 ex-Marylebone has departed; Banbury's No. 44860 is in charge. The station buildings were demolished after closure, but the platform still exists. Rugby Borough Council bought the whole of the former Great Central Railway track bed through Rugby in 1970, and it is now a nature walk: the Great Central Way. The former goods yard, west of the station, was used as a timber yard until the mid-1990s, when houses were built on it.

14 July 1965

Having brought me the 103 miles from London whilst working the 14.38 Marylebone to Nottingham Victoria, Annesley's No. 44717 transferred to Edge Hill later that month. It is seen departing Leicester Central. All I then did was cross the island platform and accrue a further 103 steam miles back to London on the 17.15 ex-Nottingham.

9 July 1965
Northampton-allocated
sister No. 44936 was
that day's standby loco
at Leicester Central.
Transferred to Colwick in
February '66, I caught up
with her a month later on
the 17.15 ex-Nottingham.

25 August 1964
This was the first of
three Colwick-allocated
locomotives witnessed
during my forty-minute
stopover at the cathedral
of steam, Nottingham
Victoria station. The once
thriving parcel business
is shown to good effect.
B1 4-6-0 No. 61299 is
silhouetted in the sunshine,
awaiting completion
of station duties prior
to departure.

7 May 1965
At the head of my
126-mile journey to
London was Bletchley's
4-6-0 No. 44909. She was
working that day's 1B97,
the 17.15 Nottingham
Victoria to Marylebone,
and, after the GC was
closed, was transferred to
Rose Grove.

7 May 1965
My only sighting of
a Robinson-designed
7F 2-8-0 Class 04/8.
Colwick's No. 63675
is held at signals
whilst working
a southbound
freight. This
forty-nine-year-old
veteran was
withdrawn the
following January.

7 May 1965
Thompson-designed B1 No. 61299 (again) passes through light engine. The grandiose former refreshment room serves as an atmospheric backdrop. She was to spend her entire seventeen years working GC line trains. In July '67 the Grantham trains were diverted to Nottingham Midland. This was followed by the truncating of the Rugby services at the reopened Arkwright Street station that September, thus allowing Nottingham Victoria, at a mere sixty-seven years old, to be closed to passengers. Eventually, the through lines, having remained open to freight a further eight months, were closed and the site, falling victim to the inevitable residential/commercial redevelopment, albeit incorporating the station clock tower, was sold.

18 June 1966

Unbeknown to us, Saturday 18 June was the last day of steam. K1 No. 62011 is seen at Alnwick preparing to work the 3 miles to the ECML station of Alnmouth with the 08.09 train. Although quoting heavy financial losses, was it more than just a coincidence that an expensive bridge would have had to be constructed for the line to cross the proposed Alnwick by-pass? A preservation group, with hopes to extend back into Alnmouth, has recently reopened the eastern section of the line.

Later that month, the steam-saturated Shrewsbury/Chester/Birkenhead services were hit, followed by the Fellsman Railtour, which traversed the Long Drag behind two Jubilees. Indeed, upon the realisation that the fast dwindling numbers of this once prolific class were becoming an endangered species, strenuous efforts in targeting the summer Saturday dated services (on which they were liable to work), resulted in catching all remaining nine NER-allocated examples by early July.

That summer a considerable amount of time was spent chasing steam on the WCML services north of Crewe, with occasional incursions into Scotland. Every weekend I, along with a group of like-minded friends, invaded the fast disappearing steam scene. We didn't always travel together, often meeting briefly and swapping notes when sighted. With the objective of travelling behind as many different steam locomotives as possible (defined as haulage bashing), many hours were spent at Wigan, Preston and Carlisle in order to corral our prey. Locations never having been contemplated visiting were visited, such as Barnsley, Bridlington, Scarborough, Rhyl, Aberdeen, Ayr and Blackpool. Glimpses of, by then rare, classes such as V2s, A2s, A4s and Flying Pigs were the icing on the cake; the LMR's last surviving Jubilee, *Sierra Leone*, being caught just eight days before withdrawal.

1 September 1966

Stanier 2-6-4T No. 42647 waits departure time at Birkenhead Woodside with the 14.45 for Paddington. She will work the 15 miles to Chester where, upon reversal, the six-coach train will be taken forward by a 4-6-0. Woodside station, once the grand outpost of the Great Western Railway, was opened as late as 1878 and replaced the inadequate 1844-built Monks Ferry station. By the time of my visit the station displayed all the signs of neglect associated with uncared for steam-age infrastructure, with soot encrusted metalwork and the feeling of dereliction. Provided with five short platforms, the rails disappeared from the terminus sharply on a curve into a deep, vertical cutting and then, almost immediately, into a ½-mile-long tunnel beneath the town. It was an atmospheric hemmed-in location where the sound of the steam locomotives moving off resounded off the surrounding high walls. A recent transfer in from Springs Branch (Wigan), this Birkenhead-allocated tank was withdrawn in March '67 upon the cessation of the Paddington services. A bus/car park now occupies the site.

25 June 1966

Wakefield's Jubilee No. 45694 *Bellerophen* readies herself for departure at Blackpool North with the 13.25 for Bradford and Leeds. Not satisfied with their acquisition of the former Central station site ten years earlier, Blackpool Council was complicit in the closure of the original North station in 1974. The former excursion platforms (some distance to the east) were now the resort's main station.

Above: **2 September 1966**
The East Lancashire Railway, fed up with sharing access to Preston's platforms with a myriad of other companies, constructed their own adjacent to the main North Union station in 1850. In the gathering gloom, LM's sole surviving Jubilee, Bank Hall's No. 45627 *Sierra Leone*, comes to a stand in Preston's East Lancs platforms with the 19.00 Blackpool North to Liverpool Exchange. Transferred from the Midlands in 1962, this thirty-one-year-old Crewe-built locomotive was withdrawn just eight days later.

Opposite above: **16 April 1968**
Having previously spent seven of her twenty-five years on Western Region territory, Rose Grove's 8F No. 48410 is seen entering Preston's East Lancs platforms with a northbound freight. Contraction of services in the '70s led to the former East Lancs platforms being completely demolished to make way for a new Butler Street entrance to the station. It was short-listed for the 2017 Carbuncle Cup, an annual prize awarded to the UK's ugliest construction building during the previous year, being likened to a deadening cake tin slapped on its side!

With the majority of us being railway employees, the travel perks associated with the job were used to their maximum. On the last weekend of that year's summer service I excelled myself with a five-night, 109-hour outing, sleeping in waiting rooms, trains and, when fatigue took over, at a variation of other locations.

Into September and, with the expected influx to the SR of six Brush Type 4s, more time was spent accumulating steam mileages with Bulleid Pacifics. Keeping an eye out for tours using unusual steam power, the Crab Commemorative Railtour was participated on in October, followed up a month later with a wonderful seven-hour, 123-mile railtour of Mancunian suburbs including Bacup, Millers Dale and Manchester Central. Finally that year, one further visit was made to the Isle of Wight railways, being closed at the year's end for electrification, regrettably not yielding any publishable photographs.

8 October 1966
No need for the *Shed Directory* walking instructions to access Goole shed: the Crab Commemorative Railtour, which had started from Liverpool, went straight there. First we see the thirty-four-year-old Hughes-designed LMS 5F No. 42942 on the turntable, the celebrity for which this tour was run.

8 October 1966
The first of two examples of the shed's mainstay of locomotives: 2-8-0 No. 90094.

8 October 1966
An imposing view of sister 1943-built No. 90030. The site is nowadays occupied by the predictable supermarket and car park.

26 November 1966
Opened by the LNWR to get out of the congested shared Victoria station, Europe's longest platform, between Exchange's 3 and Victoria's 11, was opened in 1929. Stanier No. 42644 is seen at that platform preparing to depart with the 'Three Counties Special'.

26 November 1966
Just a week before closure Manchester Travel Society organised a tour, which called here at Bacup, where I yomped across the adjacent River Irwell in the pouring rain to take this shot of the twenty-nine-year-old Trafford Park-allocated locomotive, running around her train.

26 November 1966
At Bury Bolton Street two ancient LMS tanks, Nos 47202 and 47383, took the four-coach train forward on the 22-mile onward journey to Stockport. Although closed in 1980, in connection with the nearby bus/tram interchange, it was reopened seven years later and is now the thriving HQ of the East Lancashire Railway.

1967

It was all disappearing so fast. With both the Eastern and Western Regions now void of steam-powered passenger trains, I wondered which would be next. With the drip feed of increasing conversion of steam train services on the Southampton line being turned over to either DL or EMU traction, during the early part of '67, full use of my season ticket resulted in substantial steam mileages being accumulated.

By now the only opportunity of travelling over various unusual routes was courtesy of the numerous railtours being operated throughout the country. As such, the Bridport Belle tour, with its well-documented body in the toilet and disastrous attempts at climbing Toller Bank, was embarked upon that January. Another tour, the Southern Rambler, advertised as the last steam train to Eastbourne, and routed via the Mid-Kent line, together with the Elmers End to Selsdon byway, lost to the Croydon tramlink in the '90s, was also travelled on.

22 January 1967
Whilst appreciating that Maiden Newton is still open for continuity purposes, I have included this shot of the Bridport Belle there – firstly seeing Ivatt No. 41320 at Maiden Newton with the already late-running tour.

22 January 1967
At the other end of the train sister No. 41295 is on the buffers at Bridport itself, unaware of
the task that lay ahead of her in attempting Toller Bank in falling rain. This branch somehow
escaped the Beeching Axe, but not for long. The station site is now an industrial estate
containing two supermarkets.

I had, in that March, obtained promotion to the SR (SWD) Wimbledon office –
my journey from my Kent residence now being via Clapham Junction. Envious
of colleagues who commuted in from the Bournemouth line by steam, and upon
espying the 08.16 morning Kensington Post Office train departure, when time
allowed, I journeyed on it, returning on the 08.33 en route to work. On over thirty
occasions in fact! In the process of this, I had a run with all the Nine Elms tanks
allocated there at the time.

Wolverhampton Low Level, Shrewsbury, Chester and Birkenhead Woodside,
until the March of '67, were served by express services from Paddington. With
these being steam-powered north of Shrewsbury, the last four Saturdays (together
with the final 'Cambrian Coast Express' out of Aberystwyth) were bashed. That
March, aware of imminent arrival of the 4 REP EMU sets, my greatest ever
monthly steam mileage, of 5,305, was achieved; I was effectively living on SR
trains with the occasional visits to my workplace!

Next up were the Bradford portions which, resulting from the closure of Leeds
Central, were to cease on the last weekend of April, four preceding Saturdays
therefore being spent in the area. The very last of these clashed with the final Friday
of indigenous steam in Scotland and so, taking a day's annual leave, a journey over
the Renfrew Wharf branch and, due to a lack of expected steam on the Gourock/
Wemyss Bay services, a three-shed bash in the Glasgow area was undertaken. After
then and by travelling overnight, the final steam departure, Stanier No. 44846 on
the 03.32 for Halifax, was caught out of Leeds Central just nineteen hours later.

21 April 1967
An easy five-minute walk one evening enabled me to visit Basingstoke shed and having photographed Standard 4MT 80152 upon returning to the station who should come storming up the bank but...

21 April 1967
Nine Elms Driver Porter – a favourite amongst us enthusiasts for his gung-ho attitude to high speeds over the newly fettled racing track between Basingstoke and Woking.

28 November 1965
Having taken over the 11.30 Waterloo to Bournemouth from her failed sister No. 73086 *The Green Knight*, No. 73088 *Joyous Gard* sets off from Basingstoke. The shed can be seen in the background.

7 May 1967
The final steam train to visit the Swanage branch was the rail tour depicted here. With Corfe Castle itself in the background, unmodified West Country No. 34023 *Blackmore Vale* stands patiently at the prearranged photographic stop on the branch. The station was reopened in 1995 by the Swanage Railway preservation group.

22 April 1967
Just a week prior to the closure of Manningham shed (and thus by default steam out of Bradford Forster Square) and Holbeck's Stanier 5MT No. 44852 prepares to depart with the 10.05 'Devonian'. In 1990 the line was truncated to make way for a shopping centre, and the station was rebuilt on the sidings complex, where a Fairburn 2-6-4T is shunting in the distance.

28 April 1967
Visited on the final Friday of Scottish steam, this is allegedly Renfrew Wharf station. The 07.19 ex-Glasgow Central had arrived behind Corkerhill's Standard 4MT No. 80004. With just one returning train each day, the 16.41 from Renfrew Fulbar Street (a ½-mile distant), it was little wonder passengers were scarce. DMUs took over for the remaining few weeks of the line's existence. Much of the line is now a cycle path.

28 April 1967
Once Glasgow's premier shed supplying LMS Pacifics for the WCML services, Polmadie was now just an empty shell. One of the seven locomotives in steam was Scotland's sole surviving LMS Fairburn tank, twenty-year-old No. 42274. She was specially diagrammed to work an end of steam 17.03 Gourock to Glasgow Central that evening but, not being aware of it and frustrated by the lack of steam earlier that rush-hour, we were on our way south by then!

28 April 1967
Corkerhill was the shed for the G&SWR routed trains. The only locomotive in steam at the time of our visit was Stanier 4-6-0 No. 44699, with whom we had travelled with earlier that day whilst it worked the 06.55 Glasgow Central to Hillington West. Already withdrawn, Standard 4MT No. 80128 awaits her fate – Corkerhill being her home for eleven of her eleven and a half years of existence.

28 April 1967
One of the two locomotives in steam at Motherwell shed was Kingmoor-allocated BR 9F
2-10-0 No. 92051 – a representative of a class never allocated to Scottish sheds.

22 April 1967
The elimination of duplicate city railway termini was always going to happen in those days of
the retrenchment-minded BR management, so on 1 May Leeds Central ceased to be. Just eight
days before closure, Fairburn 2-6-4T No. 42699 awaits her next call for duty.

13 May 1966
An earlier scene from May '66 shows Ivatt 4MT No. 43130 struggling up the incline (necessary to cross the Leeds/Liverpool canal) out of Leeds Central with ECS. The top of the wagon hoist can be seen on the left. The site was cleared and acquired by the Post Office and all that remains there today is the blue plaque remnant (at road level) of the aforementioned wagon hoist.

With the Bournemouth main line track now fettled in connection with the upcoming electrification, many high speeds were being obtained behind the remaining steam fleet – often being run into the ground in the process. Taking a break from them, the Three Dales Railtour that May was a wonderful opportunity to view the scenic Yorkshire Dales with a host of freight-only branches thrown in the mix. I abandoned the tour in the late afternoon, dashing north to Carlisle to obtain a run behind a Carlisle-based Britannia on the last booked regular steam train into Scotland – the 20.32 Carlisle to Perth. Although this was to cease in early

20 May 1967
The opportunity was taken at a photographic stop at Leyburn whilst participating on the Three Dales Tour with K1 No. 62005. This station, 17½ miles from Northallerton on the once 40-mile-long cross-country route to Garsdale, has subsequently been reopened in 2003 as part of the Wensleydale Railway.

20 May 1967
The furthest west we could go that day was here, at Redmire. The K1 has run around our train and is topping Sulzer Type 2 No. D5160 as the tour retraces its steps en route to Catterick. Kept open to facilitate the operation of MOD trains after the limestone traffic ceased in 1992, this station was also reopened by the Wensleydale Railway, in 2004.

20 May 1967
Another run around, this time at Catterick Bridge, sees No. 62005 about to take us around a circuit of Catterick Camp, under watchful eyes. The station was demolished soon after the line it served was closed. The site now forms part of a Richmondshire district waste tip.

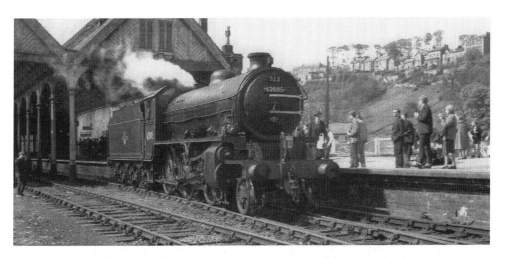

20 May 1967

The same tour also called in at Richmond. Although rail services ceased in 1969, it was re-opened (albeit not for transport purposes) in 2007 with two cinema screens, a restaurant and café-bar, an art gallery and a heritage centre.

June, the occasional extra/relief over the order was, much to the ScR authority's exasperation, dispatched north with steam. A June visit to Ashington Colliery was well supported by us, the mix of a Jubilee and a ride with an NCB locomotive being the lure. Although unfortunately losing my spectacles, in the process the NCB kindly returned them to me in the post.

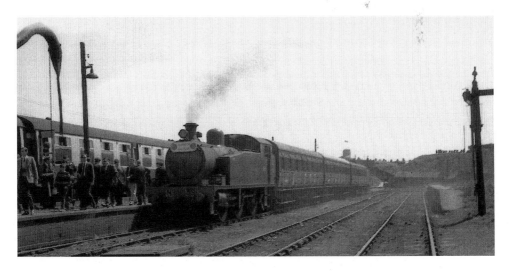

10 June 1967

The Ashington Railtour had arrived with Jubilee No. 45562 *Alberta* and all the participants were treated to a circuit of the colliery on a Paddy train, hauled by NCB 0-6-0 saddle tank No. 39. The site is now occupied by the Wansbeck Business Park.

Early July saw me aboard the final steam arrival into London Waterloo, after which, with just a handful of trains on the NER, all eyes were concentrated on the WCML. It was all coming to an end. This was to be the final steam summer. Every weekend the area was invaded by enthusiasts homing in on the wavy lined trains, a fair majority of which, even at this late stage, were steam-powered. Bereft of steam-filled weeknights, a few of us bashed the Widened Lines loco-hauled services out of Moorgate together with the Crompton-operated Oxted line trains. It didn't last long. It just wasn't the same!

***Above and below*: 15 July 1967**
The usual diet of regular train services at Keswick were normally formed of DMUs from the WCML junction station of Penrith. However, in July '67, a 09.30 parspec from Euston, in connection with the annual Keswick convention, was run, powered from Penrith with two of Kingmoor's 'Flying Pigs' – Nos 43120 and 43121. The surviving platform/buildings have been awarded Grade II status and are incorporated as part of a hotel complex.

4 August 1967

With there being a dearth of required locomotives in circulation, the opportunity to visit Lostock Hall shed was taken. Having arrived into Preston at 11.00 with No. D5712, one of the short-lived Metropolitan Vickers Type 2s, I failed to document how I journeyed to the shed – Ribble bus or taxi with others? Not equipped with the necessary permit, the foreman, upon production of our BR identity cards when requesting permission to wander around, often replied, 'I haven't seen you', thus exonerating him should any mishap befall us. It seems I didn't stay long because my next entry in my notebook indicates that I caught the 11.47 service from Lostock Hall station, itself with Edge Hill's No. 44838 working that day's 11.00 Liverpool Exchange to Blackpool North. When the L&YR opened this shed in 1881, I bet they wouldn't have thought that it was to play such a pivotal role at the end of steam in August '68.

28 August 1967

Located at the end of a 10¼-mile branch from Oxenholme, Windermere was opened in 1847 by the Kendal & Windermere Railway. It was leased in perpetuity to the Lancaster & Carlisle Railway before, in 1858, being absorbed into the L&NWR. It was the August bank holiday Monday, and Britannia No. 70045 *Lord Rowallan* had arrived with the 09.45 Adex from Liverpool Lime Street. Windermere station (actually located in the village of Birthwaite) boasted, at the time of my visit, four platforms, an overall roof and a turntable. Reduced to a single platform in 1973, the line was truncated in 1986 – the former train shed being incorporated into a supermarket.

1 September 1967
Somehow escaping the predilection most 9Fs had for wearing a coat of limescale, twelve-year-old 9F 2-10-0 No. 92056 calls at Carnforth, when it had platforms on the WCML, for a crew change. Note the nuclear flask in the consist.

2 September 1967
Opened as Morecambe in 1907, the station acquired the appellation of Promenade seventeen years later. As befitting its then title, I took the sea air by just crossing the road outside the station before boarding this 09.10 portion to Lancaster, where it would be attached to the rear of a Carlisle/Euston service, seen here with Carnforth's No. 45017. With passenger numbers falling the local council, similarly to Blackpool, persuaded the cash-strapped BR to sell them the land, truncating the line at a newly built station nearer the town a year after my visit. The station and Midland Hotel have been sympathetically retained, the former now an exhibition centre and public house. A supermarket and car park now occupy the land which was once the platforms and sidings.

The North Eastern finale at the end of September left us with just a handful of passenger trains still steam-operated, and most of those ran during the ever-lengthening night hours. One October Saturday, just to while away the time awaiting the evening Preston portions, I stayed aboard the 01.17 Manchester Piccadilly departure (steam to Guide Bridge) to its destination of Cleethorpes – returning to the WCML via Louth (closed 1970), Boston, Peterborough and Nuneaton. Railtours were now being well-patronised – they were fast becoming the only guaranteed steam-powered trains.

***Above*: 30 September 1967**
Named Barnsley for the its first fourteen years, the final Saturday of North Eastern Region steam sees Stanier No. 44971 arriving into Cudworth with the 07.06 Sheffield Midland to Leeds City. The line was closed the following January as a result of mining subsidence.

***Right*: 15 October 1967**
Accessed by the Carlisle Kingmoor Railtour, which went right into the shed, a total of 109 locomotives were copped that day, of which fifty-two had already been withdrawn. First up, alive and kicking, is Heaton Mersey's twenty-six-year-old 8F No. 48252 with a further six months of existence ahead of her.

15 October 1967
12A had, by default, become
the Britannia Class's graveyard.
Here, Brit No. 70010 *Owen
Glendower*, a former ER
Willesden and Crewe locomotive,
reposes in the sun. Withdrawn
the previous month, she had
taken me over both Shap and
Beattock banks in recent times.

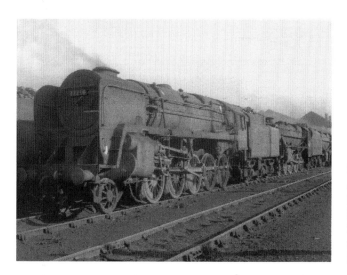

15 October 1967
A long way from her
Birkenhead home, nine-year-old
Riddles-designed BR 9F
2-10-0 No. 92234 was never
to return, being withdrawn at
Kingmoor later that month.

15 October 1967
Long-term 12A resident
snowplough-fitted Crewe-built
twenty-two-year old Black 5MT
No. 44884 is seen at rest. She
escaped to Newton Heath upon
Kingmoor's closure that December,
being withdrawn in June '68, a
month prior to that shed's closure.
Following the closure of the
yard and depot, wildlife began
to recolonise the area before it
was opened as the Sidings Nature
Reserve, under the ownership of
Carlisle City Council.

1 December 1967

Whilst Manchester Victoria station still exists this scene can no longer be seen, the Manchester Arena having been constructed over the northern section of the station. It's just after 13.00 hours and Kingmoor's No. 45259 had arrived into platform 17 with 1J42, the 12.17 portion (off the 08.25 Glasgow/Liverpool) from Preston. Newton Heath's No. 44890 is held at signals on the adjacent goods line. I was aboard No. 45259's train and we had had a near two-minute stop at Salford to regain steam pressure – the whistle having been stuck in the open position

27 August 1967

Standard Prototype 4-6-0 No. 73000 is seen at Manchester Victoria, having worked in on the portion detached at Wigan NW off the overnight Glasgow/Liverpool train. On all other days this train would have terminated at the Exchange station but with no Sunday shift rostered, Victoria it had to be. This nomadic prototype Standard 5MT, which was showcased alongside *The Duke* (No. 71000) at the 1954 Rolling Stock Exhibition at Willesden, was withdrawn at Patricroft, her fourteenth shed, in the March of '68.

1968

With a couple of exceptions, the majority of steam-hauled passenger trains in the early months of '68 ran through the night hours. This scenario, coupled with an invitation by a far more widely journeyed enthusiast colleague, led me to look to Europe to sate my steam travel addition. To this end, a ten-day pan-European trip through France to Italy and Austria certainly staved off what would have been full-on depression if concentrating purely on the British scene.

15 January 1968
Acquiring its appellation of North Western in 1924, it is included here because the present station is nothing like the one I visited in the sixties. Here, Patricroft's Standard 5MT No. 73053 waits patiently in the south bay to work the Manchester portion off the late-running overnight sleepers from Scotland. It eventually departed 347 minutes late due a tornado hitting Glasgow and a fatality south of Carlisle. During the early seventies, the run-down Victorian-era station buildings were demolished, and the track layout was re-modelled as a prelude to electrification.

25 June 1966
Chester-allocated Stanier 5MT No. 45231, in ex-works condition, is seen waiting time with the
05.35 all stations Preston to Crewe. This train, on which I was to travel on sixteen occasions,
was frequently used for running in ex-works locomotives. *Sir Nigel Gresley* and *Oliver Cromwell* were both noted after works overhaul.

18 February 1968
Having travelled overnight from the UK, hopes of steam-hauled extras, in connection with the
Winter Olympics, were dashed upon locating the depot master, who stated they were all DLs.
Perhaps taking pity on us since we had come so far, he showed us around the depot and allowed
us to cab 141R624, which had arrived in on a freight.

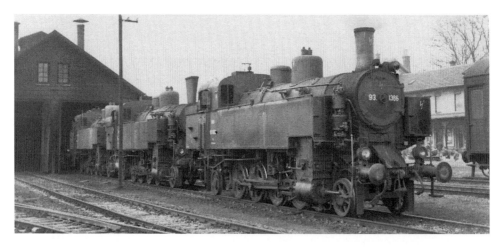

21 February 1968
With time to kill, whilst waiting for one of the somewhat sparse services operated over the mini maze of meandering Lower Austrian railways, the pivotal point of which was here at Mistelbach, the opportunity was taken to bash the shed. No one challenged us as we walked around and photographed three examples of the sixty-year-old 2-8-2T Class 93 locomotives, which monopolised the non-railcar services in the area. The central loco (No. 1417) was the only one noted to be equipped with a Giesl ejector. All bar one, now an electrified extension of the Wein Metro, of the railway lines in the area have since closed.

The one daylight train that kept hopes (for a required haulage) alive was the 09.00 portion out of Liverpool Exchange station which, upon arrival into Preston, was placed on the rear of a Manchester to Scotland service. Seemingly part of a Rose Grove diagram, locomotives from this usually non-passenger shed were very welcome. Liverpool Exchange, opened in 1850, was in fact a replacement for an earlier temporary structure just short of it at Great Howard Street. It was initially jointly owned by the L&YR and ELR. The latter insisted on calling it Tithebarn Street (its actual location) for the first nine years until its absorption by the L&YR, which no doubt caused confusion for any prospective passengers. Damage to the overall glass roof by the Luftwaffe, during the Second World War, was never fully repaired, and by the time of my visits, the ten-platformed station had a somewhat abandoned feel about the place. After witnessing Britain's final steam train in August '68, its demise was hastened when, the following year, all services excepting the Southport and Ormskirk EMUs, together with the Wigan and Bolton DMUs, were diverted to Lime Street. Six platforms were then sacrificed to enable tunnelling work in connection with the Merseyrail scheme, diverting the EMU services' direct access via Moorfields to Liverpool Central – final closure being enacted in April 1977.

My one and only non-steam railtour was travelled upon that March. A countywide tour of Kent with visits to Chatham Dockyard, Gravesend West and Tilmanstone branches, top and tailed with a pair of Cromptons, just had to be done – it was, after all, my home county. A week later saw me return to France before a further attempt in the North West for steam train catches.

9 March 1968

Having spent the early hours that morning returning from Heysham on a mix of buses and late-running Scottish sleeper services, the welcome sight at Liverpool Exchange of Rose Grove's No. 45382, working that days 09.00 Preston portion, cheered me up to no end. The frontage of the station building has been preserved and incorporated into a new office building, whilst the former station site is still largely intact and used as surface car parking.

16 March 1968

The isolated 13-mile suburban route from Paris Bastille terminus to Boissy-Saint-Leger was the last home of the 141TB 2-8-2T 1913-built class of steam locomotives. With electrification work in hand for the line to be incorporated with the RER system, a visit just had to be made. Here, the 09.00 (No. 457) and 10.00 (No. 477) push-pull services await departure time. Initially used as a concert hall and exhibition centre, the station was demolished in 1984 to make way for the Opera Bastille. The high-level approach has been retained as a promenade walk.

20 April 1968

This was Heysham Harbour, which had a complicated history of closure, relocation and renaming (as Heysham Port) and was demolished soon after my visit. Having travelled there by the 04.30 bus from Lancaster bus station, I found Carnforth's No. 44758 preparing to work the 06.15 'Belfast Boat Express' the 4½ miles to Morecambe where, upon reversal, 10A stalwart No. 45025 will take the train forward to Manchester.

Neatly coinciding with an Irish railtour, on 5 May the final steam-hauled 'Belfast Boat Express' was journeyed upon – just days before a BRB diktat, which instructed all LMR Divisions to ban steam on passenger trains with effect from the summer timetable that year, came into force. Forced to hunt for steam elsewhere, a runabout ticket in West Germany's Black Forest, together with a central France trip, were undertaken. In July, the occasional Blackpool portion out of Preston and a couple of British railtours were travelled on. Having been present on Saturday 3 August's 21.25 Preston to Liverpool Exchange, the very last public timetabled steam train in mainland Britain, I participated on one of the six steam specials the following day. West Germany and France were to see more of me from then.

Above: **4 May 1968**
A representative of the last class of steam locomotives to work in the British Isles, UTA WT 2-6-4T No. 56, brews up at Belfast York Road shed to take the Slieve Cualann Railtour the 112 miles to Dublin. 0-6-0 *Lough Erne*, the last tank locomotive built by Beyer Peacock & Co. and now preserved, albeit as a static exhibit, can be seen in the background. Steam finished in Northern Ireland in October 1970.

Opposite below: **20 April 1968**
With the normal hiatus in daytime steam trains by that April, I idled away the time with a shed bash to Stockport, just over two weeks before its demise. Completely unaware that a railtour was calling there that morning, with 9B resourcing the double-headed Stanier 5MT power, upon being unable to board it (fully booked?) I made plans to return the following week for its repeat. It was a wonderful 215-mile six-locomotive (involving the final BR 9F worked passenger train) tour, via NER metals, finishing at Liverpool. A Network Rail delivery unit now occupies the site.

30 June 1968
We had deliberately made our way to this central France location of Ussel having heard on the enthusiast grapevine that it was the final outpost of the 141TA Class. They allegedly operated the nearby Le Mont-Dore branch line trains. We were, alas, two weeks too late and the depot master, similar to his Grenoble counterpart, took pity on us and allowed us to wander around his shed. These shots, the first of which shows 141TA370, were taken in the blisteringly hot 40-degree centigrade midday heat.

30 June 1968
The miscreants missed, all awaiting dispatch to the breaker's yard.

30 June 1968
Having photographed the only live steam, in the form of 14IF189's arrival on a freight, we dejectedly made our way home. The site nowadays appears to be abandoned, albeit with the shed still *in situ*.

4 August 1968
This day will last long in the memory of those who were present, it being the very final day of British mainland steam. There were six separate rail tours being run that day and the London one I was aboard (shown here) had arrived late at Carnforth, giving the train's participants just twenty minutes to dash around taking photographs and notes.

4 August 1968

Enthusiasts were clambering over the silent locomotives, akin to maggots feeding off decaying carcases – anything detachable being secreted away within their clothing. A great many chalked embellishments adorned these fallen comrades – the most heart-rending one I read being 'goodbye cruel world'.

30 August 1968

British mainland steam had finished earlier that month and so the net (for steam haulages) had to be widened. At the beginning of a ten-day Europe-wide trip, elephant-eared 141R No. 587 readies the 13.18 Paris Nord departure at Boulogne Maritime for the 76 miles to Amiens, where an EL will complete the journey. The railwayman seen by the locomotive's side is about to escort the train through the docks complex. The Nord steam fleet were all withdrawn within two years, and the station site is at the heart of a vast urban project redefinition and has been used for various cultural functions.

6 September 1968

At Hof, situated in the north-eastern corner of what was West Germany, we had become stranded as we were unable to cross into Czechoslovakia due to the invasion just weeks earlier in line with the Warsaw Pact. Once again, perhaps as a compensatory offer to us having come all this way from the UK, the depot master permitted us to walk freely around his shed. First up are a trio of 1928-built Class 86 locomotives – used predominantly on the three branch lines emanating from the nearby town of Coburg.

6 September 1968

Then there is one of Hof's magnificently kept twenty-two 01 Pacifics, used on all the fast services radiating from there.

6 September 1968
Finally, one of the 3,000+ Class 50 2-10-0s which would appear indiscriminately anywhere throughout West Germany on both freight and passenger trains. After Carnforth the previous month, this was an uplifting scene of a working steam shed, which was to last a further five years.

19 October 1968
The Calais foreman kept his fifty-plus-year-old Pacifics in immaculate condition. The subsequently preserved 231K8 prepares to work the southbound 'Golden Arrow' out of Calais Maritime. The service was dieselised and the Pacifics condemned the following January.

April 1988

My future wife Joan waits in vain for a train at Kingscote station! Although the line between East Grinstead and Lewes was closed, in 1955 a local spinster, quoting an Act of Parliament, managed to force the SR to restore train services the following year. Kingscote, not having been part of the original Act, was not served by the so called 'sulky' service. After the eventual closure in 1958, the Bluebell Railway, from their 5-mile stretch between Sheffield Park and Horsted Keynes, reached there in 1994 and reinstated the line through to East Grinstead nineteen years later.

So was that it then? With my hoped-for target of rides behind 1,000 different steam locomotives falling just short, I think not. After imbibing on the final train over the Waverley in January '69, one last twelve-day/night bash throughout Europe the following month solved that – my 1,000th haulage being collected in the depths of a snow-covered Yugoslav plain. With vastly increasing diesel and electric mileages having to be undertaken to reach steam trains, I must admit my travels tailed off. Closures of a swarm of Lincolnshire lines, together with the Clayton West and Alston branches, were undertaken during the '70s but fall outside the remit of this book. Various short stretches of London suburban routes, usually in connection with improved transport links, were also visited during the eighties. I hope this collection has either, if the reader is of a sufficient age, bought back memories of locations visited, or, if of the future generation, enlightened them as to what they missed out on.

Acknowledgements

Without doubt my ever-understanding wife must take priority among those who have had to cope with my hermit-like existence whilst compiling this tome. Then there is my primary school teacher daughter, Victoria, who assisted me with some technical issues at this book's proof stage. One mustn't forget John Bird (anister.com) whose miracles on over fifty-year-old negatives have made them worthy of inclusion here. Finally, to the *Steam Days* magazine editor, Rex Kennedy, who, in 2004, published my first article, thus kick-starting a late life career as an author.

To view my website please visit http://mistermixedtraction.smugmug.com then select one of twenty galleries, click on slideshow and sit back and enjoy. Anyone wishing to purchase copies of the images contained therein please visit anistr. com where, under featured photographers, you will find my name and all my photographs from those five hectic steam-chasing years.

About the Author

Keith Widdowson was born to his pharmacist father and secretarial mother during the calamitous winter of 1947 at St Mary Cray, Kent. He attended the nearby schools of Poverest and Charterhouse. He joined British Railways in June 1962 as an enquiry clerk at the Waterloo telephone bureau because his mother had noted his obsession with collecting timetables.

Thus began a forty-five-year career within various train planning departments throughout BR, the bulk of which were at Waterloo but also included locations at Cannon Street, Wimbledon, Crewe, Euston, Blackfriars, Paddington and finally Croydon – specialising in dealing with train crew requirements. After spending several years during the '70s and '80s in Cheshire, London and Sittingbourne, he returned to his roots in 1985 where he met the steadying influence in his life, Joan, with whom he had Victoria. In addition to membership of the local residents' association (St Pauls Cray), the Sittingbourne & Kemsley Light Railway and the U3A organisation, he keeps busy writing articles for railway magazines and gardening for local pensioners.